CHURCHES THAT HURT

Dealing with Gossips, Manipulators, Power Brokers and Pastors Who Hurt

Churches That Hurt
Dealing with Gossips, Manipulators, Power Brokers and Pastors Who Hurt
by Dan White

© Copyright 2016 by Dan White. All rights reserved.

Scripture quotations marked (NIV) are from
THE HOLY BIBLE, NEW INTERNATIONAL VERSION®, NIV®.
Copyright © 1973, 1978, 1984 by Biblica US, Inc.®. Used by permission.

Cover Concept: Katie White
Layout & Design: Lamp Post Publishers

Without limiting the rights under copyright reserved above, no part of this publication — whether in printed or ebook format, or any other published derivation — may be reproduced, stored in or introduced into a retrieval system, or transmitted, in any form or by any means (electronic, mechanical, photocopying, recording or otherwise), without the prior written permission of the publisher.

The scanning, uploading, and distribution of this book via the Internet or via any other means without the permission of the publisher is illegal and punishable by law. Please purchase only authorized electronic editions and do not participate in or encourage electronic piracy of copyrightable materials.

Trade Paperback ISBN-13:	978-0-9985367-0-5
ebook ISBN-13:	978-0-9985367-1-2

Dedication

To my father and mother, Bob and Brenda White, who were hurt deeply by a church thirty-five years ago. They recovered and have now been faithful church members for twenty years. They walk with the Lord and have allowed the Holy Spirit to transform their lives. They have broken the bonds of various issues that have afflicted generation after generation in our extended family.

I could never express enough how much I respect my parents for the journey of healing and patience they have taken with each other over the decades.

Contents

Acknowledgments vii

Introduction ix

1. American Civil Religion and the Faithful Church 1
2. No Limits to Behavior 15
3. Ignoring a Key Scripture 23
4. The Increase of Low Grade Mental Illness 37

   Intermission I 49

5. Dictators and Passive-Aggressives 53
6. The Few, The Rotten, The Disturbed Pastors 69
7. Financial Transparency and Pastoral Accountability 79
8. Difficulty Breaking Into Social Groups 91
9. Struggling and Failing At Small Groups 97
10. You Have a Pulse? You Can Be a Member. 105
11. Pain Because the Scriptures Are Not Taught 121

    Intermission II 135

12. Discipleship and Biblical Literacy 137
13. A Gift: Standards for Christian Leadership 153
14. Transforming the Church's Staff 169
15. Excommunication Is *Not* Burning at the Stake 179
16. If You Have Been Hurt 191
17. For You, What Are the Traits of a Faithful Church? 197

    Appendix 203

Acknowledgments

Four friends turned this book from a first draft into an infinitely better draft. For the remainder of this life I owe a tremendous debt of gratitude to Warren Langer, Mark White, Pamm Fontana and Mark Daley. All four of you are true friends. Thank you.

The cover photo of the statue, "And Jesus Wept," is from Oklahoma City. In 1995, two domestic terrorists caused tremendous death and suffering there. This statue, across the street from the tragedy, reminds us that Jesus weeps when we choose to hurt one another.

When we choose to hurt one another in the church, and we all stand by and allow it to be done over and over again, we are not the church our Lord has called us to be. And Jesus weeps.

Ricky Barnard took the photo of the statue. I appreciate his willingness to give permission for its use. The cover design is by Katie White. Copy editing was by Brett Burner of Lamp Post Publishers.

Introduction

Did you pick up this book because a church has hurt you? Join the club. We number in the tens of millions now. We may even be the fastest growing demographic in the United States.

Dr. Richard J. Krejcir has studied for decades why churches fail. He writes, "The number one reason why people stop coming to any given church, (such as your church) was reported by over 91% of people who cited the significant factor or main reason as being conflict and gossip."[1]

There are new church starts in our land whose primary method of initial growth is to reach out to those who never wish to step foot in a church again because they have been hurt.[2] They try to reach people who love Jesus but don't want to risk being hurt by a church again. This demographic is so large it has become an identifiable mission field in most communities in the U.S.

---

1 Richard J. Krejcir, "Why Churches Fail: Part I." At http://www.churchleadership.org/apps/articles/default.asp?articleid=42339&columnid=4545 October 23, 2016.
2 Joanne Solis-Walker, Speaking to a Class at Wesley Seminary, Indiana Wesleyan University on July 24, 2014. The church is Nomad Community Church in Melbourne, Florida.

At River Oak Community Church in Elkhart, Indiana, a long sermon series was recently titled, "When Good Churches Go Bad." There were billboards in the city and a significant marketing campaign going after people who had been hurt by church. The sanctuary filled up Sunday after Sunday.

Churches are closing by the thousands every year. They became full of emotionally damaged, out-of-control people who hurt others. When a pastor finishes serving one of these churches, it takes years for the pastor, – and the pastor's family – to recover and heal from the experience. Some never do, and drop out of the ministry entirely.

Here's a few questions to ponder.

1. How did we get here?

2. What are the cultural and church dynamics that have brought us to this place in history?

3. Is there something wrong with our current definition of the church that allowed this to happen? What do the Scriptures say?

4. What can we do to keep the local church we attend, serve and love from going down this path?

5. What practical steps can be taken to keep our churches from hurting others?

INTRODUCTION

6. If we determine that our local church is beyond our ability to repair, how do we find a healthy church so we don't have to go through the hurt again?

An attempt to answer these questions is what this book is about.

I wish I could say I've never been hurt by a church. Maybe a completely detached academic should be writing this book so everything could be objectively examined. Then again, maybe God has chosen me to write it precisely because I understand the depth of the pain a church can inflict.

God started nudging me three years ago to begin writing. I resisted out of busyness. Two years ago God started pestering regularly and then practically yelled at me to stop delaying and get it written! I think I have some of Jonah's blood in me, but finally I was ready to stop and pour it into the computer. I didn't want to be swallowed by a large fish. I'm sure a piece of the resistance is that I didn't want to deal with the painful memories this book has dredged up.

Every name and location has been changed in the stories. Every effort has been taken to avoid identifying the innocent, the guilty and those who are a bit of both. I'll tell the stories as faithfully as I can remember them. Beyond that I'll rely on my beautiful wife, Gloria, to correct the pieces I don't remember well. More important than writing a book of historical accounts it is my hope that you will see your own similar hurts within these stories and recognize the moral in each one. Together we can decide to reform the church and make it a place that refuses to hurt people. Let us dream together for the day when our buildings for worship can once again be called sanctuaries from a disturbed and gossip-filled culture.

All Scripture references are from a New International Study Bible[3] given to me by a church in Pensacola, Florida. This Bible is beat up and has seen service on four overseas mission fields over the decades. The church was full of gossips, manipulators and powers brokers, including a patriarch of one church family who hadn't been to worship in fifteen years. I was always amazed at the power he wielded. As a youth director at the age of nineteen I watched a bold pastor named Gerald Freeman work to turn the church toward a new direction. It became a growing, healthy body and a powerful, missionary-sending church. It helped support my family overseas for many years.

My prayer is that I have heard from God, told stories from the past faithfully, offered practical suggestions and have helped to develop a new understanding of the church (one which is quite old, and biblical, as well). By doing so the hurting can stop and the church can get back to doing what she was called to do.

Yours in Christ,
Dan White
Summer of 2016

---

[3] *The New International Version Study Bible*, Zondervan Bible Publishers, Grand Rapids, MI, 1985.

CHAPTER 1

American Civil Religion and the Faithful Church

Ephesians 5:29-30
After all, no one ever hated their own body, but they feed and care for their body, just as Christ does the church – for we are members of his body.

At the age of twelve I found myself in the back seat of my family's nicest car. We were going to church. When we moved to Tampa my father promptly found a distinguished church downtown which was full of people of quality. There were doctors, lawyers and lots of local politicians.

From the small fifth floor of the church where the youth room sat, one could see Tampa Bay with ships coming and going, and all of the gorgeous mansions on Bayshore Boulevard. When we were accepted into membership, my father, who grew up dirt poor in the Southside of Chicago, said that we had now arrived. We were now with the people of quality in Tampa.

The only problem is that we lived thirty-five minutes away in the suburbs. Dressed in our nicest clothes and in our best car we were prepared to be with the upper crust. Dad gave us the frequent lecture on how to behave at church as we drove down Interstate 275 toward downtown. At that moment we were twenty minutes from home and just fifteen minutes from church. Then all hell broke loose.

My father reached into his coat jacket and realized he had no business cards with him. He roughly asked my mom if she had taken this suit jacket to the cleaners. She had. A string of expletives came out of my father. At this point my sister and I came out of the half-hypnotized states we had been in as the scenery rolled past. Something interesting was happening now.

Dad insisted that mom search the glove box for business cards. None were found and more expletives came out. None were in my mother's purse, either. In desperation my father asked my sister and me if we had any. We sheepishly said no and wondered if expletives were headed our way.

We could see the tall buildings of downtown Tampa coming closer. We were only ten to fifteen minutes from church. Muttering to himself, my father took the next exit off the interstate, turned around, and headed home. Twenty-five minutes later, now armed with business cards, we left home again. We would be forty minutes late to church, but more importantly, my father had business cards to give out as needed.

Years later, when I was sixteen, the Senior Pastor asked his wife, along with their two kids, to move out of their house. Two weeks later the church secretary moved in and lived with the pastor until the divorce was finalized and they could get married. The board of the church did *nothing*. He continued to serve the church for five more years until he accepted the pastorate of a larger church in a different city.

It took twenty-five years, but eventually that large church shrunk to a small size and then decided to close. The building was sold. Before the title changed hands to the new owner, a memorial service for First Church was held. An article about the upcoming service was in The Tampa Tribune and many former members saw it, including me. Upon arriving for the last Sunday morning service I found it difficult to find a parking space even well away from the church. The 800-seat sanctuary and balcony were packed and there was standing room only. The chairperson of the board, whose office was about to expire as the church closed, asked the packed-in congregation a question at the end of the service: "Where have you all been over the years? Where did you go?" Yet another one of hundreds of "First" churches was gone in the spate of church closures between the year 2000 and today.

American Civil Religion and the Faithful Church

I believe there is American Civil Religion and the Faithful Church[4], Holy and Universal. They are two separate entities. American Civil Religion is the fallen, politically

---

4   Avery Dulles, *Models of the Church*. Image Publishers; Exp Rei edition (1991). From Chapter 1, The Church and the True Church.

corrupt, bring your business cards, lukewarm at best, inward focused organization that hurts people right and left. It exists in almost every denomination and movement. If you picked up a book with the title *Churches that Hurt*, you have experienced American Civil Religion, or at least heard tales of it. These local congregations are dying at a fast pace in the United States, but they are hurting a lot of people as they go.

While there's a cross on the sign outside and another inside in the large auditorium, only pieces of the Gospel of Jesus Christ are given out. People in the seats are not discipled, and the moral bar for entering church leadership is shockingly low. When the winds of culture blow, these organizations quickly follow. American Civil Religion is church with a small "c" and is a large phenomenon in our land.

The Faithful Church, Holy and Universal, is the bride of Christ. It is where two or more are gathered together and the Holy Spirit chooses to breathe the life of God into the gathered community. Addicts find healing. Marriages are saved. The wind of the Holy Spirit makes itself apparent regularly. Because the Spirit blows through it there is life and growth and transformation. The Faithful Church can meet in a sanctuary, a high school auditorium or a living room Bible study. Because it is centered on Christ, it wraps itself around the great truths found in the Apostles' Creed and the Holy Scriptures.

It beats vibrantly in the community in which it is planted. Life is found in Christ and because the Faithful Church is centered on Christ, the Holy Spirit is generously given to the communities around the Faithful Church and they are transformed. The Faithful Church is unified in Christ across denominational lines. The Faithful Church is a minority group in dying denominations and the majority in growing denominations and movements.

American Civil Religion is morally challenged and good at hurting people. After being in it for years, the overall morality and truthfulness of its membership decreases. One of my pastoral students in Peru chose a research project and came up with a written integrity test complete with moral situations. In a weak, dying church he gave the test to those who had been in the church a year, five years and ten years. The lowest scores came from the members who had been there the longest.[5] Yes, morality decreased with every year of membership.

Ethics become more relativistic with every Sunday morning speech that is given. People get hurt and leave. Purity becomes a word that is not tolerated by those who say they view tolerance as their highest value. In short, anything is tolerated.

Those who speak their dreams of returning the church leadership to purity are derided as self-righteous and intolerant. Quickly the organization rids itself of those who speak of Christ's modern disciples as needing to seek holy living because God is Holy. Tolerance of the newest political movement or unbiblical lifestyle is touted as a proud accomplishment. "The closer the church gets to the culture, the better," they say. Their solution to membership decline is to become more acceptable to the culture.

---

[5] Quispe, Marcos, *Etica en la Iglesia Metodista*. Bachelor's Thesis, Probitem Library, Huancayo, Peru.

What the Supreme Court says becomes official theology. Members in the pews slowly come to see the world in the same way their highly-paid pulpit princes do; as many shades of gray with no absolutes being revealed from a loving, teaching God. The Scriptures are slowly dismembered in twenty-minute speeches, one each Sunday. With every visit to the building, members have their morality lowered until it reaches the low level where the church leadership lives. Of course people will get hurt and leave. Gossips, manipulators and power brokers are welcome in American Civil Religion.

The Faithful Church is a light that transforms those who worship there for the better. People come and hear the inspired words of Matthew, Mark, Moses, Isaiah, Luke, John and Paul through the power of the Holy Spirit and through the instrument of the preacher. The preaching forever changes the people. Instead of a piece of the Gospel being given, the Word of God is presented in its entirety. Some weeks it washes over the hearer and is instantly experienced as a blessing. Some weeks it hits between the eyes and makes us struggle with its truth all week. We are called out of our comfort zones and asked to purify an area of our lives where we were truly satisfied in our apathy or our addiction. In the Faithful Church, a follower, a disciple, is made sharper with every visit to the place of worship or small group meeting; whether that sharpening is easy to experience or painful to endure.

Meanwhile, American Civil Religion is concerned with itself. The choice of music matches what the *membership* wants. The community is irrelevant. Outreach is limited to three or four small events per year to help the church feel some justification for its existence. The local Rotary or Lion's Club does more for the good of the community and the wider world than the congregation does.

Karl Marx had a problem with the church. He called it the opium of the people.[6] For once Marx was right. Opiates put people to sleep and help them to become addicted and self-interested. So does American Civil Religion. Programs are focused on the needs of the membership and there is a sense of sleepiness to the place.

This inward focus begins with self-absorbed clergy leadership. When there is a vote on their own salary, health insurance, retirement benefits or reimbursement budgets the clergy is actively persuading or even stacking the committee involved.

The Faithful Church is concerned with its surrounding community. Because Christ died for the Faithful Church *and* for the world, there is a passion to help the least of these. I don't use the word passion lightly here. It is a prime motivator of all of the Faithful Church's decisions. Worship lyrics are chosen to the glory of God and the music is chosen to invite the community in.

American Civil Religion has no intentional discipleship program. Those who wish to be members are welcomed with open arms. Another member on the roles makes the pastor look better to the regional leader who influences

---

6 Karl Marx and Frederich Engels, *The Communist Manifesto*. International Publishers Co. (2014). Marx actually wrote that religion is the opium of the people but I'm using a bit of writer's license to apply his famous phrase here to American Civil Religion. The Faithful Church, which Marx may never have seen up close, enlivens the soul, moves people outside themselves and causes people to deeply care about the poor. If Marx had experienced the Faithful Church positively transforming communities, he would have fallen in love with it.

promotions. Once they are members, no further teaching, mentoring or discipleship is required, and often is not even offered.

The Faithful Church takes its lead from the Early Church and disciples its new people. One surviving eighteen-hundred-year-old document speaks of a program of discipleship for new converts that was normally three years long.[7] The modern Faithful Church does one-on-one mentoring before membership to deal with addictions and life-destructive, hidden behaviors. Holiness, based on God's nature and God's holiness, is gracefully emphasized. Expectations are clearly, graciously and lovingly expressed. Those new to the life of the congregation stumble and fall but the Faithful Church helps them to get back up and begin their faith journey again.

The Faithful Church is a place of healing while American Civil Religion knows how to hurt people regularly. Is it any wonder that tens of millions of people have left American Civil Religion feeling wounded? Emotionally healthy people flee it.

Because our society does not differentiate between American Civil Religion and the Faithful Church, some judge all congregations to be alike and swear off organized religion. The Faithful Church ends up being rejected by more and more people in society because both it and American Civil Religion have the word "church" on the sign outside.

---

[7] The Apostolic Tradition (Possibly of Hippolytus of Rome. The authorship is debated). At http://www.bombaxo.com/hippolytus.html October 23, 2016. The exact phrase in Chapter 17 is, "Catechumens will hear the word for three years. 2Yet if someone is earnest and perseveres well in the matter, it is not the time that is judged, but the conduct."

AMERICAN CIVIL RELIGION AND THE FAITHFUL CHURCH

Maybe you are feeling that this first chapter is judgmental in nature. Martin Luther, John Wesley and a host of others have called the churches of their time corrupt and fallen. They recognized the difference between the fallen church and the faithful church. A man named Athanasius of Alexandria in the 4th Century was exiled five times because he kept talking about the difference between the Faithful Church and the false church.

The difference between the two has always been with us. Paul refers, angrily in Galatians, to parts of the church he, himself, planted just a few years earlier. The best translation of Galatians 1:9 is that he tells the promoters of that which is false to go to hell. Less controversial translations have Paul telling them to be eternally damned.

The Old Testament prophets railed against those who said they were of God but were not. Jesus our Lord strongly condemned the Pharisees. The Scriptures are full of a dichotomy between the True and the False. We should not be surprised that it is with us today. As Spener wrote in 1675, "The precious spiritual body of Christ is now afflicted with distress and sickness."[8]

In the second chapter of the book of Revelation, seven churches are mentioned. John is receiving the vision that makes up the book of Revelation while he is in exile on the Island of Patmos. Prior to his exile he served these seven churches. God speaks and is deeply unhappy with five of the seven. Only two of them are being the churches they need to be.

---

8 Philip Jacob Spener, *Pia Desideria*, Translated by Theodore G. Tappert, Fortress Press, 1964, Page 31.

There are lampstands representing the churches. When God is unhappy with one of them there is the threat that its lampstand will be taken away. That object which can hold a lit lamp, lit with the fire of the Holy Spirit, may be taken away. If it is, the power of the Holy Spirit will be removed from the congregation. Excitement will die. Lives will cease to be transformed. The young and the old will no longer come to the faith.

Does your church still have a lampstand? Are visits from the transforming Holy Spirit still frequent? Do you leave the church feeling transformed on a regular basis? If not, the possibility exists that your church's lampstand is no longer there. If God doesn't see the gathering of people as a church, then it really isn't one.

Writing in this manner can be viewed as judgmental or divisive. This is especially true when our culture highly values tolerance. When a person differentiates between what is of God and what is not, they are seen as judgmental. *Within this climate the False flourishes.* Gossips, manipulators and power brokers are able to take the reins in congregation after congregation.

And people get hurt. It is now a national phenomenon.

And Then There's the Mix

It would be so easy if one building had the words, "American Civil Religion" on the sign and another said, "Faithful Church." Because we are fallen human beings there will always be a mix of the two in most congregations.

AMERICAN CIVIL RELIGION AND THE FAITHFUL CHURCH

Dr. Archibald Hart, the renowned Christian psychologist, once sarcastically challenged a group of pastors to place a large neon sign above the main entrance to their church. It would say, "This week we are 70% dysfunctional." It would be changed as the church's level of dysfunction went up or down. At least this way we would be honest with visitors, he said.[9]

So the first stop on our journey toward stopping the hurting is to realize that American Civil Religion and the Faithful Church have always resided side by side.

With increasing frequency, enough of the Faithful Church flees a local congregation so that those who hurt others take over and are free to act as they please. The first-time visitor doesn't even think about returning. With the flight of the faithful from within their midst these churches often close within a decade.

It is with a clear definition between the False and the True that we can move on and ask ourselves the questions: How do we strengthen churches that are part way down the road toward American Civil Religion? What can we do to strengthen the church we love and help it to stop hurting people?

A Massive Transition

We are in the middle of a massive transition within Christianity in the U.S. The old is dying and the new is growing and strengthening. Denominations and schools

---

9   Hart, Archibald, During a Doctor of Ministry course titled, *Minister's Personal Growth*. Fuller Seminary, Pasadena, CA, Fall 1996.

of thought that have led Christianity since before the American Revolution are dying out.

Fuller Seminary has long been known for strong academics combined with an emphasis on what works, practically speaking, in growing local congregations. It has recently produced a "5 Year Strategic Vision." It includes a key paragraph:

> Mainline Christianity in the United States needs reinvention. The fundamentalist and modernist alternatives of the twentieth century have become barren, and the ecclesiastical institutions that were built during that era are struggling for direction. The days of American civil religion are gone, though vestiges remain in some places. Many Christians presume denominational irrelevance and decline.[10]

What a statement! The old is dying. Have you ever noticed that when some people die they don't do so gracefully? They kick and struggle and verbally hurt those around them.

Organizations do the same. Part of the hurt that stems from the church today flows from the painful and growing realization that three nearby churches have already closed and that theirs may be next.

---

10 Fuller Seminary Board of Directors, "The Task Before Us. A 5 Year Strategic Vision." May 8, 2015.

Questions for Reflection

Here are a few questions about the Faithful Church and American Civil Religion. Feel free to add your thoughts.

From what you know about First Church, Tampa, remembered through the eyes of a teenager, is the surrounding community worse off or better off for the closure of First Church?

_____
_____
_____
_____
_____

Did the Kingdom of God in Tampa grow smaller when it closed?

_____
_____
_____
_____
_____

When have you experienced American Civil Religion? When have you experienced the Faithful Church?

_____
_____
_____
_____
_____

Every year 4,000 churches close in the U.S.[11] How many would you personally guess were real, Faithful Churches and how many were American Civil Religion and helped the cause of Christ by their closure?

_____
_____
_____
_____
_____

---

11 Krejcir, Dr. Richard J., *Statistics and Reasons for Church Decline*. At http://www.churchleadership.org/apps/articles/default.asp?articleid=42346&columnid=4545 October 23, 2016.

CHAPTER 2

No Limits to Behavior

James 3:5b, 6
Consider what a great forest is set on fire by a small spark. The tongue also is a fire, a world of evil among the parts of the body. It corrupts the whole person, sets the whole course of one's life on fire, and is itself set on fire by hell.

We know there are people in churches who are comfortable hurting other Christians. They do it frequently and unabashedly. They feel the freedom to do so because no one has placed boundaries on their behavior and insisted they stop.

A district superintendent in Central Florida, serving an old and large denomination, once said to the board of a local church, "Some of you have done things here that would get you fired from your jobs. Somehow you feel comfortable doing them in the church."

The Superintendent's comments were partly directed at a leader (let's call him Mike) who felt it was time to change pastors. In that church there is a committee who makes recommendations to the Superintendent about when it is time to make a pastoral change. Mike called each member of this committee and expressed his opinion. The committee met and decided to recommend keeping the pastor.

So far, so good. Mike had an opinion and he expressed it. He had not gone to the pastor yet to express his concerns but he had followed the bylaws and contacted those who represented the local church to the Superintendent. Unfortunately, Mike did not stop there.

After having his concerns rejected by the committee Mike began to call each and every member of the church, starting with those whose last name started with A and working his way to the end of the church directory. Mike was emotionally recovering from losing his job a few weeks before and the anger and extra free time led him to his calling spree. He began conversations with the question, "Don't you think it is time to change pastors?" and then answered his own question by listing off the litany of complaints he had.

A church that had grown from eighty in worship each weekend to 130 in the eighteen months since the pastor arrived suddenly stopped growing. Political camps formed. Spreading the Gospel of Jesus Christ in a loving way to the community was placed on the back burner while the parties went to war.

In the midst of all the turmoil, the regional superintendent met with the board. She laid down the line about acting in the church in ways that would get a person fired at work. Her voice was stern. Regrettably, her resolve was not.

NO LIMITS TO BEHAVIOR

Mike, and his brother-in-law, moved on to e-mail. E-mail addresses were in the church directory. They began to send out scurrilous attacks regarding the pastor and the new path he was taking the church.

One woman (let's call her Jenny) decided to print off the e-mails and file a formal charge against the two men under the denomination's bylaws. She sent a letter to the Superintendent asking for the two men to be brought before a regional trial on the charge of "undermining the ministry of a pastor," a chargeable offense in the bylaws. Potentially this offense could result in a regional trial which could remove the two men from positions of church authority for a given period of time.

The response of the Superintendent was not to call for a trial even though she knew exactly what they had done. It was not to ask the two men to step down voluntarily or even to speak with them one-on-one about the inappropriate emails. The Superintendent's response was to inform Jenny that those parts of the denomination's bylaws had not been enforced in over a hundred years and there was nothing she could do. Her talk was tough but her follow up was not.

The local church was a war zone and shrunk quickly. Even life-long members left, as did all of the new arrivals. The pastor, seeing no possibility for the Kingdom to move forward and feeling very wounded, requested a move. Not long after, he left the denomination.

This denomination's official statistics show it is closing 1.8 churches a day across the United States and has lost four million members over the last four decades. The lack of enforceable boundaries for the laity, and for many pastoral transgressions, is one of the reasons.

I Want, Therefore It Must Be

There has developed within certain congregations in the U.S. a sense of *no limits* when it comes to getting "what I want." The end (my desires) justifies the means. If I want to sing a solo in the worship service, then who is the worship pastor to tell me I need to practice more or don't have the voice for it? If I come up with a great idea for an outreach ministry, who is the pastor to tell me "No" or the finance chairperson to tell me the church doesn't have the funds? This means WAR. All the stops come out, gossip becomes a useful tool and half-truths are good enough as ammunition.

I will get what I want in the life of the church or others will pay a price for getting in my way. As I save my church from those other leaders who are dead wrong on today's issues of tremendous importance to me, three families will leave the church. When tomorrow's issue comes up, I'll fight just as hard and just as nasty. More will leave the church, but at least I got what I knew to be the right thing for the church. The end justifies the nasty means.

As painful as it is to watch, it is even more painful when the manipulator gets their way. They know they got their way because of their willingness to have no boundaries and they are even more likely to repeat the behavior the next time they want something.

In this decade, decisions in congregations are often *not* made by searching out God's will in prayer. Many decisions are no longer made by a process resembling democracy in the congregation. Instead, decisions are made by manipulators who are the most emotionally disturbed members of the congregation and who have the filthiest of methods for getting what they want. Healthy, moral people leave and the manipulators have an even stronger hold on the congregation.

And another church closes ten years after the political wars begin. American Civil Religion is following down the path of many of our state and federal candidates for elected office. Dignity and integrity, while disagreeing with one another, has left the arena of combat.

Write Your Own Story Here

At this point every experienced church person could write his or her own story of pain and hurt where the person who inflicts the pain goes undisciplined. People are hurt and Kingdom growth is impacted.

Please write that story here.

_____
_____
_____
_____
_____

A Prayer for the Hurt

Lord, you didn't want it to happen. It was not your will that I was hurt. Like Jesus on the cover of this book, you wept when the church hurt me. Help me to forgive the person or persons who hurt me.

In the Sermon on the Mount you call me to pray for my enemies. I'm not sure this person is an enemy but they hurt me and I am angry. Lord, I commit to pray for this person every day until I know in my heart that I have forgiven them. Grant me the strength and resolve to carry through with these prayers. Help me to find the freedom that comes from the act of forgiveness.

Take this hurt and transform it into something positive. Help me to be a better servant. Help me to be a better leader. Help me to find the strength to graciously confront those in the church who callously hurt others.

• • •

There is another story that just has to be told. It will knock your socks off.

Dr. Steven Lawson, who many say is the strongest preacher in the country right now, tells this story of what happened in his large church as he preached through the book of Job, one chapter each week:

> I preached Job 1. I preached Job 2. And as I prepared to preach Job 3 all hell broke loose in my life and ministry. Someone broke into the church that I pastored and secured the membership list. They went and bought a P.O. Box and wrote a four-page letter indicting me and charging me with being one who believes in the sovereignty of God in salvation.

NO LIMITS TO BEHAVIOR

A ballot was in that letter. You were to check one of two boxes. Either you were a Baptist or a Calvinist.[12]

Can you imagine what was going through that person's mind as they broke into the church office to secure the membership list? They chose to divide a church over the issue of whether or not John Calvin was correct in his writings in the sixteenth century about predestination! Somehow he rationalized it because he thought he was right. They didn't write the elders and express their discontent. They had to break into the church office in the middle of the night and then write a four-page letter to the membership. Just printing and mailing the letter must have cost over $2,000. All over a point of theology and a desire to see a pastor removed.

It doesn't stop at pastors, either. I've seen vocalists go to war with each other in the rumor mill of the church because they both wanted to be the primary singer for worship services to Almighty God. *And no one came alongside them and told them to stop.* We tend to fear people who are willing to use the rumor mill and be manipulators so we don't confront them – and the behavior continues. People get hurt, and across the country another ten thousand people leave the church and decide that organized Christianity is not for them. It hurts too much.

• • •

---

12 Steve Lawson, 2010 Shepherd's Conference, General Session 8: *The Invisible War.* March 5, 2010. Found at http://www.shepherdsconference.org/media/details/?mediaID=5239

Jim had been at the church for fifteen years. A lot of people knew him in the nine hundred-attendee-per-weekend congregation, but not many knew what his role was on the elders' board. One day the pastor decided to talk about Jim's job description:

> When we have someone get out of hand and they begin to tell rumors and gossip about someone else, Jim is the person on the Board who we send their way. He goes into their living room in a gentle and incredibly loving way. He tells them what the issue is and how they could have handled it. Some people say "thank you" and never do it again. Others get offended and leave. We all enjoy coming into this place, this sanctuary from the world, in part, because of Jim.

Jim got a nice standing ovation for his work over so many years. The pastor announced Jim was moving to Florida to retire, then he preached fervently from the Scriptures for the next forty-five minutes about how the entire congregation needed to pick up Jim's work and continue it in the future. He preached about speaking softly but directly. He preached about tough grace in difficult moments.

I checked on this Nazarene church last week. They are now averaging over 1,300 per weekend. I can't prove a cause-and-effect relationship between their stance on gossip and their growth, but I certainly suspect it.

This is the Faithful Church.

CHAPTER 3

Ignoring a Key Scripture

Matthew 18:15
If a brother sins [against you][13],
go and show him his fault, just between
the two of you. If he listens to you,
you have won your brother over.

Matthew, who walked with our Lord and Savior Jesus Christ for three years, has a discourse on living a healthy life within the Kingdom in the eighteenth chapter of his Gospel. The passage above is about the beauty of going one-on-one to a person who has sinned or offended us before we take it to the gossip mill or Facebook.

Matthew and eleven other men walked long distances with our Lord, talked, ministered and lived together for three years. They did everything together. It was intense fellowship that probably bred interpersonal conflict.

---

[13] The oldest manuscripts of the New Testament in Greek, Vaticanus and Sinaiticus, do not include the phrase, "against you," in verse 15. This makes sense as other scriptures call us to defend the poor and seek justice. We do not approach others only when they have sinned "against us," personally. This phrase appears to be added to the text as the Bible was copied in later centuries. At: https://www.reclaimingthemind.org/blog/2011/08/textual-problem-study-matthew-1815/ October 23, 2016.

While in seminary for three years, I spent a great deal of time with my classmates but I went home to an apartment. I can't imagine sleeping in the same room every night with a group of twelve disciples, eating together, ministering together, walking together…everything, together. In the midst of this close fellowship, Jesus says that if you believe someone has sinned or offended you, go to the person and discuss it, "just between the two of you."

Matthew 18:15, the verse for this chapter, immediately follows the parable of the wandering sheep. The shepherd leaves the ninety-nine sheep behind and goes all out to bring the one lost sheep home. The life of the Faithful Christian is marked by caring deeply when someone falls into sin, and he will do anything he can to see a brother or sister restored. The Faithful Christian doesn't gossip about sinners, but instead focuses on what is best to restore the lost sheep to the community

Verse 15, commanding us to go one-on-one to someone who has sinned or who has offended us is based on restoration. We keep it one-on-one because we want to see the person restored to God and restored to full fellowship and friendship.[14] Going one-on-one restores relationship. Gossiping about someone's offence destroys relationship and adds more sin to the situation.

When we offend someone, as we often do, the offenses fall into various categories. Almost all are solved by Jesus' words to go to the person one-on-one.

---

14   MacArthur, J. F., Jr. (2006). *The MacArthur study Bible: New American Standard Bible.* (Mt 18:15). Nashville, TN: Thomas Nelson Publishers. This thought is contained in the commentary section printed below Matthew 18:15.

IGNORING A KEY SCRIPTURE

- You may have been trying to make a joke and the person didn't realize it was a joke. Maybe it was a joke in poor taste in order to lighten the mood. The offended person comes to you and you explain it was meant as a joke. Your belief system doesn't run that direction; it was just in jest. You apologize, and the relationship resumes its normal course, maybe even strengthened by the healthy interaction. Going one-on-one to the person worked.

- You may have been distracted or in a hurry. Something popped out of your mouth when it was moving but the brain was not fully engaged. It is not exactly sin, but someone was offended. The offended person comes to you in private, you explain your true feelings on the matter in a more careful way and the relationship is strengthened. Of the original twelve disciples, I can see Peter engaging in this one. Before Pentecost, his mouth often began before his brain engaged.

- There may have been a mishearing of what you said. Jimi Hendrix is known for having once sung, "*'Scuse me while I kiss this guy*" in the song Purple Haze. What the lyrics on the song sheet said was, "*'Scuse me while I kiss the sky.*" If someone is offended, he comes to you and you explain what you actually said or intended to say. Sometimes it is that simple. Going one-on-one to the person first, rather than to Facebook, works.

- You may be dead wrong on an issue. You spoke and stated clearly exactly what you believe. After the person comes to you in private and discusses why he feels you are wrong, you come to your senses and change your mind. Going one-on-one to the person works. Even if it doesn't, it was the biblical first step.

- You may have stated what you actually believe clearly and precisely. The offended person comes to you in private and your reasoning sways him. The relationship is strengthened. Going one-on-one to the person worked.

- You may have spoken clearly what you believe and the offended person comes to you in private and shares his concern. After much discussion you agree to disagree because the issue is really not about sin but about how each defines the wise way to handle the situation. Again, it worked! Fellowship in the body of Christ remains strong.

For the vast majority of interpersonal conflict and dealing with possible sin, this magnificent verse works. When it rarely doesn't work, and someone really did sin but is unwilling to admit it, Jesus gives us verses 16 and 17 about taking another Christian with you for another conversation, and eventually to the leaders of the congregation:

IGNORING A KEY SCRIPTURE

"But if he will not listen, take one or two others along, so that every matter may be established by the testimony of two or three witnesses.' If he refuses to listen to them, tell it to the church; and if he refuses to listen even to the church, treat him as you would a pagan or a tax collector." (Matthew 18:16-17)

In my life, at least 98% of interpersonal conflict is resolved by going privately to the Christian brother or sister. Going to another person one-on-one simply works for maintaining relationships and keeping Christian fellowship solid.

Do you know what *doesn't* work to protect relationships in a group? When organizations go bad, and people get hurt in churches, it is almost exclusively when Matthew 18:15 is not followed and people go to everyone around them with the issue before they go to the person who offended them.[15] It is the right conversation with the wrong person. Trust is destroyed, embarrassment sets in and emotions run hot. Misunderstandings or easily resolved issues end up with three families leaving the Body of Christ and vowing to never step foot in a church again.

This leads us to the proper understanding of Matthew 18:15. Should we take it literally as a command or as a general teaching with wisdom in it? Dr. James Efird, a renowned biblical scholar from Duke University, taught a way of figuring out which interpretation of a particular

---

15 "In the church's intense fellowship, such sin is perilous indeed, regardless of its exact nature." Elwell, W. A. (1995). *Evangelical Commentary on the Bible* (Vol. 3, Mt 18:15). Grand Rapids, MI: Baker Book House.

scripture was the right one. Some interpretations are possible but not probable. Others are highly probable. So let's look at the possibilities for Matthew 18:15 and see which are probably the best applications. Grab a pen or pencil and circle the ones that are good applications of Matthew 18:15, in your opinion. Place a big X over the ones you don't feel are God's will:

A) If I trust the person and know they will react well, if it will be safe and comfortable for me, I will speak to them privately. I dislike confrontation and I get a tummy ache so I'll follow Matthew 18:15 and go one-on-one with the person if I feel safe with her or him.

B) I should use this verse to confront every person on every issue, even interrupting them mid-sentence to correct what they have said or where I think they might be going with the sentence. I bring truth to the world by correcting every wrong I see. I'm glad God has made me the arbiter of good and bad and given me a personality that almost enjoys conflict.[16] I'm also glad God gave me Matthew 18:15 to theologically support my habit.

C) I am really upset but I'm not sure how the person will react. I need to go talk to two friends about it before talking to the original person one-on-one.

---

16 France, R. T. (1985). *Matthew: an introduction and commentary* (Vol. 1, p. 278). Downers Grove, IL: InterVarsity Press. From the section on Matthew 18:15-18.

IGNORING A KEY SCRIPTURE

Matthew 18:15 will need to wait until my own thoughts are straight in my head. Maybe I should form it as a question on my Facebook page or other social media and ask my thirty-seven 'friends' whether or not I should be upset about this. This isn't gossip. It is helping me to think straight. Then I'll decide whether or not to go to the person one-on-one.

D) I was tossing and turning last night about what the person said yesterday. It is obviously bugging me and will be an obstacle to a healthy relationship with them. In love and graciousness, after prayer and maybe even fasting, I need to meet with the person and start with, "I haven't spoken to anyone else about this but I was troubled when you said it yesterday. Can you tell me more about what you meant to say?"

E) When choosing leadership in the church we look for spiritual maturity. If someone has not shown the ability to approach a fellow believer directly and lovingly, without talking to others first, then they have not shown the maturity to be a Christian leader or teacher. Being able to resolve interpersonal conflict in a healthy, biblical way is what we are looking for in church leadership.

F) We interpret one scripture through the lens of other scriptures. Because so many passages talk about gossip as a sin, this verse is the opposite of gossip. It is what we are supposed to do instead of gossiping. It is a command from Jesus more than it is a suggestion.

G) Leaders in the church, lay and clergy, have the responsibility to assure the smooth functioning of the Body of Christ. When I see this verse flagrantly broken by a member, leader, staff person or pastor, I have a responsibility to go privately to the person and lovingly express my concern about unbiblical behavior, especially if I see them doing it more than once. If I do not, the body will not function, as it should. By accepting a role in leadership I'm accepting this responsibility to speak directly to gossips and manipulators in the church about their behavior. It will not be an enjoyable part of church leadership, but I want my church to be healthy.

Circle the letters above that you believe are the proper interpretations of Matthew 18:15 for today and place an X over the bad interpretations.

If you circled B or C as a proper interpretation, please go and speak with your pastor and think through this carefully. A healthy congregation does not need someone who constantly corrects others or who abuses social media before they finally get around to speaking with the person one-on-one.

A is not the ideal (going to a person only if I feel they are a safe person). There are many people who have had

IGNORING A KEY SCRIPTURE

physically or verbally abusive parents, spouses, bosses or other life experiences. These life experiences lead them to the conclusion that lovingly addressing a situation one-on-one can be dangerous. Everything in their experience base tells them not to risk it! When they ask for someone to be with them during the meeting for safety's sake it is a good sign they are someone who has been treated badly in the past and is very conflict-averse.

We owe it to the proper functioning of our congregations to be approachable to people who would circle A. People should feel safe bringing a concern to us, especially if they fit in this category.

The church is for healing. The church is for growing and overcoming our past. Long-term, those who circle category A need to accept the help of the Holy Spirit, pray, fast, seek help and overcome their fear of conflict. Until they do this healing, to place a person who circled letter A into a position of leadership in the church is not going to allow the church to function as well as it otherwise would. We love these hurt people but elevating them to leadership is not doing them, or the church, any favors.

Answers D, E, F and G are great answers. Matthew 18:15 needs to be taken literally and respected by any congregation that takes the phrase "Christian Fellowship" seriously. As a friend of mine used to say, Christians need to start putting on their big boy pants. It comes down to an issue of maturity. It is not easy to pray, ask God about a situation and ultimately ask for a meeting with someone when we know it will be uncomfortable at the beginning. It might even end up extremely uncomfortable. Welcome to part of what it means to be spiritually mature.

Pastors need to preach this verse and small group leaders need to teach it. There are few verses more applicable to life in the 21st century than this one. Social media has made it imperative we bring this verse to the forefront as well as its correct interpretation.

Leaders need to be chosen based on their proven track record with regard to it. If someone handles their Facebook page like a juvenile, why should they be a Christian leader?

If a friend or member of the congregation breaks this teaching of our Lord, they need to quietly be pulled aside. Until the relationally destructive nature of this behavior is confronted frequently and regularly, by each of us, the culture of the church will remain sick, and in some places toxic, to the life of the congregation. Thousands of churches have closed in the last decade because this one verse was ignored in their life together.

Elder boards and administrative board members need to understand that one of their roles is to confront the manipulators, power brokers and gossips of the church and ask them to stop. This is especially true if the person is a fellow elder or board member. Nothing hurts a church more than gossip and dysfunction at the top leadership level.

The church in the United States needs to grow up regarding this issue, or see the culture around us continue to mock the church as nothing more than a good place to get hurt.

IGNORING A KEY SCRIPTURE

Questions for Reflection

What do the elders or administrative board members in your congregation do when someone breaks Matthew 18:15? How could they lovingly confront manipulators and gossips?

_____
_____
_____
_____
_____

How do you personally react when a person begins to tell you of a third person's sin when you are not involved in the situation?

_____
_____
_____
_____
_____

What would it sound like to ask if they have spoken to the person who offended them, yet? Write out sample words you could use to cut them off quickly when a person engages you in gossip.

_____
_____
_____
_____
_____

How can you grow your personal actions to promote a healthy culture for the congregation and discourage gossips, manipulators and power brokers to continue? What are you already doing well on this front?

_____
_____
_____
_____
_____

Jeanine was furious at her principal. At faculty meetings teachers had been chewed out in front of the rest of the faculty. This had happened at least once a month. A general spirit of disrespect coming from the administration to the faculty made everyone less enthusiastic about coming to work and teaching the kids.

Jeanine, a sought-after Spanish teacher, decided to accept a position at another school to avoid the tense situations and regain the joy of teaching, which was why she was willing to work in a relatively modest-paying field. After she turned in her resignation at the end of the school year, two district staff persons asked for an exit interview to find out why she was leaving.

Jeanine made an interesting choice based upon her Christian commitment. She went to the principal and told him every reason why she was leaving. Then she went to the exit interview and told them nothing. It was the principal who had offended her and she was not going to speak to anyone else about her concerns. One side of her wanted to be angry and vindictive, but she consciously chose not to be.

IGNORING A KEY SCRIPTURE

Jeanine kept in touch with a few of her fellow teachers from the school and they told her what a change there was in the principal the next academic year. He was choosing to be much more respectful of the faculty. It doesn't always work out this way, but Jeanine had followed her personal interpretation of Matthew 18:15.

This is the Faithful Church. We follow the teachings of the Holy Spirit given through St. Matthew both inside the church and in our dealings outside the church. We let God transform people's hearts. Our job is to act as we are called to act.

CHAPTER 4

The Increase of Low Grade Mental Illness

Luke 9:1
When Jesus had called the Twelve together, he gave them power and authority to drive out all demons and to cure diseases.

The church has always been a bathtub. People come into the church dirty with sin and problems. Our job is to love them enough to disciple them and offer experiences where the Holy Spirit can transform and heal them.

Today, those stepping into the church's bathtub are different than they were three decades ago. This is impacting how often people get hurt in local congregations.

Get ready to understand troublemakers in your congregation better. The former editor-in-chief of the *New England Journal of Medicine*, Marcia Angell, states,

> The tally of those who are so disabled by mental disorders that they qualify for Supplemental

Security Income (SSI) or Social Security Disability Insurance (SSDI) increased nearly two and a half times between 1987 and 2007 – from 1 in 184 Americans to 1 in 76. For children, the rise is even more startling – a thirty-five fold increase in the same two decades.[17]

If you ever suspected that some of your fellow churchgoers had mental illnesses, congratulations, statistically you were correct! One in every seventy-six in our society has been diagnosed and is receiving federal financial support because of their mental illness. How many more of those seventy-six are diagnosed but not on federal support? How many more of the seventy-six should be diagnosed but they are not? How many more of the seventy-six would not be diagnosed but they have a mild issue they have not dealt with?

According to Angell, "An astonishing 46 percent (of Americans) met criteria established by the American Psychiatric Association (APA) for having had at least one mental illness… at some time in their lives."[18]

If the total number of SSI and SSDI dependents is multiplying by two-and-a-half times over twenty years then the number of troubled members in our congregations is surely going up, as well. We are not in Christian fellowship with the same type of people we went to church with thirty years ago.

---

17 Angell, Marcia, "The epidemic of mental illness. Why?" At http://www.nybooks.com/articles/archives/2011/jun/23/epidemic-mental-illness-why/?page=1. From the June 2011 issue. Read on October 23, 2016.
18 Angell, Marcia, *The epidemic of...* (2011)

THE INCREASE OF LOW GRADE MENTAL ILLNESS

Why, you ask? The number one reason Angell gives is side effects from the many, many pharmaceuticals we now take, especially the psychotropics (those prescriptions that attempt to cure mental illness). Also, there are far more prescription drugs used in our society to deal with our physical issues. Each of them has side effects and many impact mental health in a negative way.

First come the psychotropics. Bruce Levine, in *Why the Rise of Mental Illness*, argues that mental illnesses are over diagnosed and then treated with strong psychotropic drugs. The result is that people on these powerful drugs, which some of them never needed in the first place, end up with even more serious mental health issues because of the drugs. In fixing one supposed mental issue, other mental issues are created.[19]

Second come the drugs for physical problems. According to the Center for Disease Control, 48 percent of us took a prescription drug last month.[20] These drugs have an impact on our mental health according to the websites of the drugs themselves.

Here's one from Chantix's own website:

> Some people have had changes in behavior, hostility, agitation, depressed mood, suicidal thoughts or actions while using CHANTIX to help them quit smoking. Some people had these symptoms when

---

[19] Levine, Bruce, "Why the Rise of Mental Illness?" At: http://www.madinamerica.com/2013/07/why-the-dramatic-rise-of-mental-illness-diseasing-normal-behaviors-drug-adverse-effects-and-a-peculiar-rebellion/ From the July 2013 issue. Read on October 23, 2016.

[20] Centers for Disease Control and Prevention, "Prescription Drug Use Continues to Increase," at http://www.cdc.gov/nchs/data/databriefs/db42.htm

they began taking CHANTIX, and others developed them after several weeks of treatment or after stopping CHANTIX.[21]

Are there any teenagers in your church taking Accutane (isotretinoin) for acne? An article on Drugwatch.com states:

> From 1982 to May 2000, the FDA received hundreds of reports linking isotretinoin use to depression, including 37 suicides, 110 hospitalizations for depression or suicidal behavior, and 284 cases of non-hospitalized depression. Roche responded to the reports of depression and suicide in 1998 by adding a warning to the medication's label stating that Accutane could cause psychiatric disorders.

The side effects are so bad that Roche stopped manufacturing it in 2009. The generic version is now available.[22]

On the other hand, the kids in your youth group don't have as much acne!

Start listening to the television ads for pharmaceuticals. When it gets to the end of the ad they start talking fast and telling you about the side effects. Many of them relate to depression, mood swings and other psychiatric issues.

I am a strong supporter of Christians seeking help from well-trained and capable Christian counselors and psychiatrists. We live in an age where our people can get help from

---

[21] Side effects explained on the official Chantix website at: http://www.chantix.com/side-effects-safety-info.aspx   July 11, 2015.

[22] Drugwatch.com article on Accutane. At: http://www.drugwatch.com/accutane/ July 11, 2015

THE INCREASE OF LOW GRADE MENTAL ILLNESS

issues ranging from bipolar disorder to chronic depression. There is much to be thankful for in modern medicine.

What should not happen is for our Christian brothers and sisters to be quietly placed into the hands of these medical professionals with no care from the Faithful Church. Let's leave the social stigma behind and admit to our Tuesday night small group Bible study that we are taking a new drug and admit that it sometimes has side effects. Ask the group to tell you if they notice a change in your personality after you start taking the new drug. Let's be a true community in real, deep fellowship instead of lonely, closeted individuals who want to present a perfect image within our American Civil Religion church buildings. The reality is that 46 percent of us are taking these drugs.

Is Bill, the volunteer treasurer, still exactly the same Bill after his doctor put him on two new prescription drugs? Is that why he had a loud, angry outburst when Maria asked for a reimbursement of thirty-six dollars? Now Maria has left the church. Is a Christian leader who loses 150 pounds due to a Lap Band surgery of the same emotional makeup as he was six months ago? When Jane's doctor changes her depression medication will Jane react to every situation the same way she did before?

When we discuss people in churches hurting others this portion of the discussion begins to boggle the mind. None of us really knows how much serious psychotropics and day-to-day medical prescriptions are affecting the way our fellow Christians or ourselves react to interpersonal stress, but something has changed, and more people are getting hurt in the church.

How do we as leaders, lay and clergy, react to this new reality? How do we remain understanding when leaders go through emotional changes in their lives and, at the same time, protect the congregation from getting hurt? Each of us may arrive at different conclusions, but here are some questions to contemplate:

Questions for Reflection

Bill, a long-serving leader in the congregation, goes on a new prescription or undergoes a medical procedure, and then has an angry, irrational outburst at Maria. After Maria decides to leave the church, how do we react as church leaders?

_____
_____
_____
_____

Jose has been through discipleship training and leadership training. His small group is growing well and he is ready to come onto the elder board or administrative board. Is it appropriate to ask Jose to voluntarily tell the pastor if he has ever been diagnosed with a mental illness and for a list of his current prescription medications? Why or why not?

_____
_____
_____
_____

THE INCREASE OF LOW GRADE MENTAL ILLNESS

Mary is ready to be a new staff person with the title *Director of Children's Ministries*. Do we ask her about any history of diagnosed mental illness 1) during the application process, 2) once she is the leading candidate, 3) at another time, or 4) never at all? Why? Is privacy a strong biblical concept?

_____

_____

_____

_____

Javier is in the middle of the ordination process. Should Javier be asked about his history of mental illness and for a list of his current prescription medications? Why or why not?

_____

_____

_____

_____

Real Christian Fellowship

Beloved Brothers and Sisters, we live in a different age now. We need real Christian fellowship more than we have ever needed it. I'm not talking about going to a spaghetti dinner and chatting with the people around the table. Real Christian fellowship is much deeper.

John Wesley, the great reformer of the 1700's called Christian fellowship a grace, much like the grace of receiving Holy Communion.[23] The Holy Spirit flows through

---

[23] Outler, Albert C. and Heitzenrater, Richard P., editors, *John Wesley's Sermons, An Anthology*. Abingdon Press, 1991.

real Christian Fellowship challenging us and transforming us.

Wesley's small groups asked each other questions when they met together each week in their small group. Here are a few of them in their original old English:

- Has no sin, inward or outward, dominion over you?

- Do you desire to be told your faults?

- Do you desire to be told of all your faults, and that plain and home?

- Do you desire that every one of us should tell you, from time to time, whatsoever is in his heart concerning you?

- Consider! Do you desire we should tell you whatsoever we think, whatsoever we fear, whatsoever we hear, concerning you?[24]

How beautiful it is when the Faithful Church goes back to asking each other questions like these each week, allowing the Holy Spirit to transform us through Christian Fellowship. Discipleship and holiness become high values and people are transformed.

---

[24] John Wesley's Discipleship Accountability Questions, At: http://www.tgcresources.com/dons-blog/john-wesleys-discipleship-accountability-questions/ July 11, 2015

THE INCREASE OF LOW GRADE MENTAL ILLNESS

Because of the modern issue of mental illness and pharmaceuticals, it is possible we need to add a question to our voluntary, modern accountability groups:

- Have any changes occurred in your life that makes you question your emotional or mental health? Are there any pharmaceutical drugs that have possible emotional side effects that we, your Christian friends, should be looking for?

Until our society passes through this time it is best that we stick closely together in Christian fellowship. We hold one another accountable. We ask the hard questions. We don't allow one member of the Body of Christ to hurt another.

On a personal note, this chapter originally stems from working with three church staff members over the last ten years who were deeply committed to gossip and manipulation. I cannot count the number of people who left these churches because of these three leaders. One church went from 750 each weekend in worship to 350. Each of the three leaders was taking prescription medications for emotional issues.

Two would make jokes such as, 'Don't mess with me today! I didn't take my meds!' The rest of the church staff knew it was not a joke and we dreaded those days. I once found myself, after a staff meeting, offering to drive the person home to get their meds.

I have *not* learned from these experiences that we should avoid having church leaders, lay and clergy, who are taking medications. This would rob the church of high quality leaders given to us by Almighty God. I have *not* learned that state and federal laws should be broken when interviewing applicants for staff positions and having them list their medications (though I would argue that an ordination process is not a hiring process in most traditions).

I *have* learned that voluntary openness and honesty about the possible side effects of medications and the state of one's emotional health should be an open topic during the leadership selection process, when legally possible, and ongoing while the person is a leader. This means leadership at all levels within the congregation. As leaders we voluntarily open ourselves to accountability regarding our mental health.

I *have* learned that I never wish to have a church leader, paid or unpaid, that is not active in a personal accountability group. I don't have to know what gets said each week in the group, but I want to know that each Christian leader, paid or not, is holding themselves, their personal purity and their emotional lives accountable to other Christians.

I *have* learned that under no circumstances should biblical standards for behavior be changed because we feel sorry for someone on medications or have misdefined the concept of grace so that a dozen people leave the church hurt because we had "grace" on one leader with mental health issues. As leaders, we serve the people of God. Period. Leadership is a responsibility and a privilege. It is not a right. In many situations a person simply needs to step out of leadership for a time.

THE INCREASE OF LOW GRADE MENTAL ILLNESS

Christian fellowship means we love one another and hold one another accountable, no matter what.

• • •

Jorge Acevedo and Matthew Hartsfield are two of the most amazing pastors I have had the pleasure of meeting. Jorge pastors a 7,000+ per weekend church in Cape Coral, Florida. Matthew pastors a 2,000+ congregation just north of Tampa.

They have both been in an accountability group with other servants of our Lord for twenty-five years. When something significant happens in a group member's life, such as an illness or a life crisis, the others are there for them. Each month they gather together to hold one another accountable.

Speaking at a conference in 2015, they laid out the need for accountability groups and the blessing it has been in their lives. I recommend this hour-long video wholeheartedly. It will change your life. Voluntarily holding one another accountable is a beautiful act.

https://youtu.be/JEXlF43WqWw

This is the Faithful Church.

Intermission I

It would be nice if they brought back intermissions in movies like they used to have. It was a nice way to stretch, take a break and contemplate.

The Faithful Church is so beautiful. Much of this book is about the need to reform the church that has fallen and now hurts people far too often. God has placed a reminder in my life in the middle of this writing process about the incredible value of the church.

Life Together by Dietrich Bonhoeffer is an amazing, short book that reminds us of the infinite beauty and value of the Faithful Church. It was written in Nazi Germany while Bonhoeffer led an underground and quite illegal seminary for the Confessing Church that stood against Hitler. Later, Bonhoeffer was martyred. As he wrote *Life Together* he knew that any day could be the end of his life on this earth. He came to value the Faithful Church very much:

> The prisoner, the sick person, the Christian in exile sees in the companionship of a fellow Christian a physical sign of the gracious presence of the triune God. Visitor and visited in loneliness recognize in each other the Christ who is present in the body; they receive and meet each other as one meets the

Lord, in reverence, humility, and joy. They receive each other's benedictions as the benediction of the Lord Jesus Christ. But if there is so much blessing and joy even in a single encounter of brother with brother, how inexhaustible are the riches that open up for those who by God's will are privileged to live in the daily fellowship of life with other Christians![25]

Let us never forget our goal. We wish to see the Faithful Church remain true and be strengthened even further. We wish to see congregations within the fallen church find the true path, strengthen, and no longer hurt people.

Ten years ago, I taught for a few weeks in an underground seminary in Cuba. While many churches choose to register with this historically horrible government, thousands of others continue as illegal churches. Half of my students had already spent two years in jail for leading unregistered congregations. If the government had found our class I would have been immediately deported to the comforts of the United States. My students would have served two years in a Cuban jail. Those with a record of disobeying the government in service to our Lord would have served much longer.

Those Cuban pastors were so hungry for the deeper Word of God. They were so ready to sacrifice. It was the sweetest fellowship of the Faithful Church I have ever experienced.

---

[25] Bonhoeffer, Dietrich, *Life Together*. Harper One, 1954, Page 20.

INTERMISSION I

I pray daily for the Faithful Church in our nation. I pray daily for the fallen church. I pray that every Christian in this land is able to understand the sweetness of true Christian fellowship and understand how beautiful the Body of Christ can be.

CHAPTER 5

Dictators and Passive-Aggressives

2 Corinthians 11:19-20
You gladly put up with fools since you are so wise! In fact, you even put up with anyone who enslaves you or exploits you or takes advantage of you or puts on airs or slaps you in the face.

As an overseas missionary to a Latin American country, I was charged with educating and training pastors in a remote district for a struggling denomination. There was a national leader of the denomination and his son, who was a district leader overseeing fourteen local churches. These fourteen pastors lived in fear of the district leader in part because the region had a forty percent unemployment rate and they did not wish to lose their jobs as pastors. My wife and I got to see how fear-based followers react to a leader with a dictatorial heart.

The district leader, let's call him Augusto, was following a long line of Latin American dictators in the 1970's, 80's and 90's. The thinking was that strong leadership was necessary because the problems were so grave, and the goal of raising people out of poverty so important, that people needed to sacrifice their human rights so the countries could progress. In government or in the church, we often hear a rationalization of dictatorial powers so good can be done for the people or so the Kingdom may expand and churches grow. Unfortunately, it is also a recipe for dictatorial hearts to seize power and abuse people in the church.

Eventually, an investigative committee from the national church was sent to look into Augusto's leadership in this remote district. They asked a lot of questions and I learned a great deal about fear-based followers and passive-aggressive behavior.

When people live in fear they tend not to directly confront a leader. Instead they find little ways to get back at the person. Often it is through procrastination, stubbornness or gossip. The key is that it is a way of showing one's aggression and anger. It is simply done without ever directly addressing the person and the inappropriate actions they have done. It is passive because there is never the feared direct conversation but there is a clear desire and will to get back at the person. That's where the label "passive-aggressive" comes from. Obviously, neither the dictatorial, abusive behavior nor the passive-aggressive responses are biblical approaches.

A lot of people get hurt in the church when this cycle begins. The leader, the follower, and the twenty people around them, all get hurt.

Augusto had a few weeks' notice that the investigative committee was coming. He met with pastor after pastor and district leaders of the laity to ask what he had done and what they intended to say.

The committee arrived and began interviewing each district pastor and myself. This was a matter for the national church, so as a missionary I did not voice my opinion regarding Augusto, but I did testify that I had translated between him and the leader of a two-week work team from California. Eight hundred and sixty dollars was handed to Augusto with the intention of it being used for Christian education in the district. The money never made it onto the district's financial statement as income.

I never thought of my testimony as courageous. I had addressed the issue with Augusto personally and received many threats from him in return. The strongest was that his father, the national church leader, would not be pleased with my testimony, as it would embarrass the family name. For me it was simply testifying as to what I had seen.

The area of learning for me in that very stressful situation was the actions of the fourteen young, fear-based pastors who had grown up in a passive-aggressive society that could never directly confront those in power who have a dictatorial heart. They originally expressed enough concern *about* Augusto when they were at national conferences that an investigative committee was sent to the district. Once the committee arrived and their testimony would become public record, they completely clammed up and said nothing.

When Augusto was in the room or would know what they had said, there was silence. When they were safe to speak, they would tell story after story of embezzlement, threats and abuse of power. A dozen pastors had already left to serve other denominations. Hundreds of people had been hurt and the reputation of the churches in the communities they served had been seriously compromised.

People from the U.S. love to assign blame when they hear stories of corruption and abuse of power overseas. I encourage you not to do so. It can quickly turn into judgmentalism and a sense of cultural superiority. Neither are deserved and neither are helpful.

My reason for telling this story is that I see this dictator/passive-aggressive response repeating itself over and over in local congregations here in the United States. A lay person has a problem with the pastor, real or imagined, and goes to everyone *except* the pastor with their concern. They block the pastor's agenda for growing the church through procrastination or not supporting key events. Leading a congregation turns into the act of herding cats. Congregations are split in two when associate pastors carry off thirty percent of the congregation and the pastor and associate pastor never did sit down and really share their hearts openly and honestly with each other. Perceived dictators and passive-aggressives are alive and well in the U.S. church, just as they are overseas.

Chances are your mind has already picked out a few guilty parties in your own past. Experienced pastors could write down a list of passive-aggressive laypersons whom they are still trying to forgive deep down in their hearts. Laypersons could write down the names of one or two pastors who they feel abused their authority, acted like dictators and whom they are still trying to forgive. Anyone who picked up a book titled *Churches That Hurt* can probably write an extensive list of names.

Don't.

When we arrive at the last chapter there will be suggestions on how to heal from these experiences to forgive those in our past. For now, let's figure out how to stop the cycle before it is repeated and we get to relive our past experiences once again.

Pastors:

- You are intimidating. While you do not see yourselves as dictators, there are those in every congregation who will see you that way. You stand on the platform most Sundays and bring the Word of God to the people. Few men and women have that much power. Depending on your church's bylaws, you either have direct power over budgets, staff and the direction of the congregation, or you have enormous influence over these areas. You are a person of power.

- Pray every day that you will not fall to the enemy's traps and abuse that power. With power comes abuse, and prayer can help stay your hand before you fall into temptation. If you abuse your power, people will get hurt.

- Maintain your spiritual disciplines of prayer, fasting, real accountability to a small group, retreats, and other disciplines which bring you into the presence of God. These bring a sense of humility to your ministry, and no one will view you as a feared dictator if you are humble.

Jesus was the most powerful, forceful, strong-willed and effective pastor of all time. No one refers to him as a dictator because he was humble. His humility came from his constant retreats and communion with the Father. Pastors, do not neglect the spiritual disciplines, for humility is the byproduct of practicing them.

- The door must be kept open to hearing people tell you what you probably don't want to hear, true or untrue about your leadership. If you are too busy or too feared, no one in the congregation will come to you when they are upset. They will go passive-aggressive instead. If enough members do this, the work of the church will come to a grinding halt. Mention from the pulpit that your door is open. Welcome people and do not get defensive. If you do, your reputation as someone to be feared will spread rapidly. Some statements you hear from these voices will result in changes to your approach. Others can slide off like water off a duck's back. Both must be welcomed, and the person thanked for coming to you. If your door is truly open, then more will come *to* you and fewer will gossip *about* you.

- Some of your laypeople, including staff, are damaged. They grew up under abusive parents or live

DICTATORS AND PASSIVE-AGGRESSIVES

under abusive spouses or bosses. They have received ample reason, in their minds, to react to people in power with passive-aggressive behavior. They need healing and they need messages from the pulpit inviting them to that healing.

- Until they are healed, they need you to go to them whenever possible. If you hear someone is upset with you, seek them out. Don't let them engage in continual passive-aggressive gossiping. Go and listen and share your thoughts in a non-defensive way. If they gossip after that, then the leadership of the church (not you, pastor, but the leadership you have trained up) needs to deal with them biblically and appropriately under Matthew 18:15-17.

    They are damaged, and they number in the tens of millions in our society. Failing to refine your skills in working with this large and growing swath of the population means being an ineffective pastor.

- If you really are a pastor who appreciates a fear-based set of followers doing what you want them to do whenever you crack the whip – get out of the ministry. Stop being a pastor today. Write your letter of resignation. You are part of the reason why people get hurt in the church today. You are doing far more harm than good.

- Finances need to be transparent. The church's bookkeeper or accountant may come up with a complicated monthly financial report. Once completed, someone needs to simplify it so the average layperson can interpret it. Then it gets posted on the website for all to see. If you do not engage in intentional transparency you will not have the trust of the congregation and the passive-aggressive response of the less mature members of the congregation will be the withholding of tithes and offerings and many other spiritually immature reactions.

- Intentional transparency, the spiritual disciplines and humility are as vital today as they have always been for effective Christian leadership.

For Lay Persons:

- It is time for all of us to grow up. Gossips and manipulators are hurting too many people. If this is you, stop. If you have listened to one and not stopped them mid-sentence, do so next time. If you have allowed the church to hurt people and have not stood up against it, start doing so. Laypeople *and* pastors are getting hurt. The communities we live in are viewing us very poorly, and it is time to become proactive in fighting this plague within the church. Pastors cannot fight this modern day scourge alone. It is the role of the laity.

- The moment you decide to go passive-aggressive instead of courageously walking into your pastor's office and sharing your concern with grace, you have hurt the church. Talking to everyone except the person who has offended you is sinful gossip, and the Holy Scriptures do not condone it.

- Do not rationalize that *any and all means* are acceptable to get rid of a certain pastor. The methods you use to get rid of the pastor who has offended you will be known by many of the candidates who might be your next pastor. You may end up with a very small pool of unqualified candidates if you succeed in getting rid of your current pastor by questionable methods.

- Using *any and all means* to get rid of a pastor results in your church becoming known for infighting and gossip. The community will know about this reputation, and it can take decades for this bad reputation to go away. Your actions will result in a drop in first-time visitors.

- If you have a concern about a pastor, a staff person or a leader, go directly to the person who concerns you. It is the biblical way to resolve conflict. If you are unwilling to do this, know that the gossip you engage in will hurt the church as much as or more than the possible concern you have about the person.

- If you come to feel strongly that your church needs a new pastor or a leader of the laity needs to step down, bring your concerns to the person first. If you are ignored, ask for a copy of the bylaws. Determine who should appropriately be informed of your concerns and any evidence you may have. Remain quiet except to those who are supposed to hear these concerns. Then trust in the Lord and let go of it. You have done what you can do. It can take many months and sometimes even a year for something to happen. If you cannot stay because you are too upset by what has happened, find another healthy part of the Kingdom of God in which to worship and participate. Do not deal with evil through unbiblical means.

- Do not live in fear. If fear is keeping you from going to someone who has offended you or is hurting the church, then your motivations come not from God but from the enemy. Only the master of hell works through fear. Pray for the courage to go appropriately, lovingly and gracefully to the person – in private.

- If you fear this process of directly, assertively and lovingly going to someone, examine your own past. You may be a damaged person due to your past. We all are. Take a break from church leadership, pray, get help and heal. Because interpersonal conflict comes with church leadership and membership, there must be healing of the past before you can effectively help to lead a church.

DICTATORS AND PASSIVE-AGGRESSIVES

- Don't go passive-aggressive and withhold your tithes and offerings. The book of Malachi calls it stealing from the Lord (chapter 3). It hurts the universal church's ability to grow and meet the community's needs. There are too many weak churches because of this behavior. Don't use God's tenth of your income as a power chip in a poker game, or you may wish to look under the table and see who's really running the game. Unless there is outright darkness and evil in the church's finances, do not withhold your tithe.

- Don't put up with a lack of financial transparency in your local church. Let your opinion be known to the pastor and every board member or elder who will listen. If there is still no transparency, consider attending a church with transparent finances. Secretive finances are a sign that an abuse of power may be taking place.

- Be willing to confront gossips in the church. They may be enjoying the rush of power they feel when they gossip. They may feel taller when they cut others down. They may be passively-aggressively getting back at someone whom they perceive has hurt them. They may be experiencing the rush of adrenaline that comes with vengeance. They may be mentally ill. Whatever their motivation, they need someone to invite them to have a cup of coffee or tea, or a walk around the community. The church exists to bring that community to Christ. Gently let them know how much damage they are doing.

- If every church has just five percent of its people committed to lovingly speaking with immature gossips, that church has the ability to turn around and grow. If it does not, then no other church growth strategy will allow the congregation to survive more than a couple of decades. The culture of gossip in our nation wants to come in. If we do not keep it out, then it will destroy our congregations, one by one.

Accountability for All

- Human beings tend toward abusing power over others whenever possible. So let's make it less possible.

- If your congregation is elder led (meaning a group of elders make key decisions together) then each and every elder needs to be under the spiritual authority of someone else. We grow together and we hold each other accountable. If you are beginning to gather and hold too much power, then your accountability partner, who is inside or outside the congregation, can bring it to your attention.

- If your congregation is pastor led, then a free and independent person or group needs to be asking questions once a month about the pastor's spiritual disciplines and potential abuses of power. Pastors can open themselves to small groups where accountability questions are asked of each other regularly. This will not remove all abuses of power, but it will remove the majority of them from the pastor-led model.

- If your church is staff led (where the staff comes together to make key decisions) then each staff person needs spiritual accountability in their lives, no matter how busy they are. There needs to be a regular time for reflection and voluntary accountability.

- If your church is led by an administrative board, then you have one of the greatest challenges of all. When a board grows beyond eight people, there is tremendous temptation to separate into political camps. Then the power games begin. Every few months, someone in spiritual leadership needs to remind the group of the need for unity, and that no one person should be allowed to gather too much power. If political camps begin to grow, then this gets addressed earlier rather than later. Each person must be in an accountability group which checks their prayer and devotional life, or they will not be invited to serve another term.

- In short, no one becomes a dictator in any of these settings because no one wants the hurtful repercussions of a system that allows the temptation toward the abuse of power to constantly hover over the congregation. With any of these systems that involve human beings, the possibility of the dictator/passive aggressive cycle is an open door to the meddling of our enemy. Sooner or later he'll walk right through the door and people will get very hurt.

- Because the temptation is always there, in elder-led, pastor-led, staff-led and administrative board-led churches, each of us needs to humble ourselves before the Lord, and before each other, to keep power in check.

- George Washington was an amazingly powerful man in his time. Anytime between the end of the American Revolution and his last days in office as President, he could have announced his desire to be King for life, and a large segment of the population would have supported his decision. He chose not to. He knew that a system of checks and balances was better for his new country. He voluntarily chose to allow his power to be limited.

- If you are a layperson or an elder with too much authority because everyone keeps handing it to you, give it back. If you are a pastor or a staff person with too much power, delegate it out. Make yourself accountable. Disciple others. Mentor others.

DICTATORS AND PASSIVE-AGGRESSIVES

Train others. As soon as possible, delegate and spread the authority out. It is the only way to avoid the dictator/passive-aggressive cycle which ends up hurting and chasing off so many people.

CHAPTER 6

The Few, The Rotten, The Disturbed Pastors

Jeremiah 23:1-2
"Woe to the shepherds who are destroying and scattering the sheep of my pasture!" declares the LORD. Therefore this is what the LORD, the God of Israel, says to the shepherds who tend my people: "Because you have scattered my flock and driven them away and have not bestowed care on them, I will bestow punishment on you for the evil you have done," declares the LORD.

Pastor Tim just couldn't stop. Something inside him made him relate to women in strange ways. From the pulpit he made insulting jokes about his wife and no one laughed. They always seemed intended to put her in her place, a place not very high. A regional leader in the denomination was called in when he made a highly inappropriate sexual comment to the female children's director in front of a group of church members.

Pastor Tim had already brought one congregation to half its original size. Then he brought this congregation from 250 per weekend down to three dozen.

You may ask: Did Tim's denomination require him to seek counseling? Yes. Did he open himself to the counseling, mend his ways and take a new path? No. Was he transferred across the state to a new and unsuspecting third congregation? Unfortunately, Yes.

Cops occasionally protect the wrong actions of fellow cops, and Bishops occasionally protect the wrong actions of fellow priests. It can be the same in any field. When it happens in the church, the hurting goes on.

• • •

I have a great many fears going into this chapter. I fear someone who has a disagreement with their pastor will start calling them a disturbed pastor or a mercenary pastor even though they are anointed, called and committed to the Kingdom. I fear someone will take this chapter and condemn a pastor who is simply asking for a pay raise so they can put their kids through college like everyone else in the congregation.

Too many pastors are already emotionally beat up and discouraged. I would never want to add to those experiences. If you are a layperson, please realize that pastors get hurt, too; sometimes very badly. Pastoral burnout is a major ailment in our land. Please don't add to the hurt by calling a certain pastor a disturbed pastor without very, very good reason to do so. With that said, here we go with

THE FEW, THE ROTTEN, THE DISTURBED PASTORS

a very difficult topic that has to be touched on to cover the topic of *Churches That Hurt*.

• • •

We cannot deny that a few pastors and church staff bring emotional pain and suffering into the lives of others on a regular basis. We need to explore what the church can appropriately do to stop the majority of the hurt from happening.

Compared to one member hurting another member, when pastors go bad their ability to hurt is multiplied by a factor of 10. Part of the hurt in the church today is that we are not doing enough to deal with troubled pastors early on.

Serial Predator Pastors can range from pedophiles to those engaging in continual sexual harassment to serial adulterers to Jim and Tammy Faye Bakker's financial fraud in the millions of dollars in the 1980's. Every local church, movement and denomination needs a section of its bylaws dedicated to grave, unrepentant sin on the part of the paid staff.

There may be situations where restoration to leadership five years later is a possibility, depending on the issue or issues. More often than not, the person needs to heal and serve the Lord as a layperson for the rest of their lives. There is no lack of dignity in serving the Lord as a layperson. Christian leadership is a responsibility, not a right. Weak and unbiblical definitions of grace, which allow another dozen people to be gravely hurt in another church, are not acceptable.

As the Roman Catholic Church has discovered, the only true solution to the issue of dealing with serial predators is to allow laypeople into the decision making process once the behavior is discovered. History has shown us, in the Roman Catholic Church and in Protestant denominations, that there are moments when clergy leadership does not deal with clergy sin appropriately and in a way that protects God's people from further hurt.

For those involved in a call system, where the local church decides who will be their new pastor, inappropriate transfers are not a significant issue because the laity are already involved in hiring the pastor. Then there are tens of millions who worship the Lord in appointment-based denominations. When high-ranking clergy determine who the next pastor or priest will be, laypeople should not put up with these regional leaders simply moving serial predator pastors to another church full of unsuspecting victims. High-ranking clergy who do so are in need of being removed from their positions or possibly being prosecuted to the fullest extent of the law if the transferred pastor violated the law. Yes, it was the serial predator pastor who gravely sinned. It is equally offensive when they are simply transferred to a new set of victims.

Mercenary Pastors are in it for the money, the power over others, or the prestige. Symptoms may include constantly looking at larger churches as their goal for being in the ministry. The work done in their present church is

THE FEW, THE ROTTEN, THE DISTURBED PASTORS

not for the sake of the Kingdom but instead is to create a springboard for a future jump.

Jeff in North Carolina worked eighty hours a week, every week, because he wanted to one-day pastor a large downtown church with "First" in its name. His third wife was discussing separation with him because of neglect. Instead of complimenting his work ethic, the leaders of the church should have talked to him about values and set boundaries on his workload.

Faithful Hispanic pastors can all tell stories of mercenary pastors who convince an English-speaking congregation to support them with a salary. The "pastor" can't tell you anything about the Holy Trinity or that there are four gospels in the New Testament. They take the salary, and when a representative from the English-speaking congregation comes for a visit they gather every relative and friend they know to show up and be the congregation on show day. It is funny how they remain at twenty to thirty people year after year. Because of the language barrier these mercenary tricksters have taken advantage of thousands of congregations. Committed and truly-called Hispanic pastors would benefit from the resources that are given to those mercenaries.

When the draft boards called on young men to serve in the Vietnam war, going to seminary was a way out of the draft. No one really knows how many men ended up in the ordained ministry, not because of a call from God, but from a desire to escape the draft.

The only solution to mercenaries is to ask a lot of questions before hiring a pastor and call their references and work history supervisors. If they are transferring from another church, call the previous church's lay leadership.

Pastors are human beings living in a fallen society. Even a pastor who starts strong and faithful may fall and become an **Addicted Pastor**. This may result in strange behavior, including embezzlement on expense reimbursements as they struggle to meet the ever-increasing demands of their addiction.

At the end of Chapter 4 we discussed each Christian leader being in an accountability group at least once a month. Hard questions about how sin is attempting to come into our lives are asked of one another in these groups. At a time in history when so much sin can come into our lives so very easily through technology, it is time we begin to consider these accountability groups as essential to healthy Christian leadership. Elder boards, pastoral oversight committees and hiring committees have it within their authority to ask a pastor if they are in an accountability group each week or each month.

These oversight groups may even ask a pastor to provide the list of questions that group members ask of each other at each meeting. Their answers need to be confidential, but a transparent pastor will be willing to share the questions asked at each meeting to show that it is a real accountability group. Healthy samples include:

1. What is the condition of your soul?

2. What sin do you need to confess?

3. What have you held back from God that you need to surrender?

4. Is there anything that has dampened your zeal for Christ?

Accountability groups are the best defense against addiction and a key part of healing from them. A longer list of potential questions for real accountability groups is found in the Appendix at the end of this book.

In our present decade it is crucial that every Christian leader, clergy and lay, join an accountability group. This is very different than a small group Bible study because of the questions that are asked of one another. Having each Christian leader in one of these groups can save a lot of people from a lot of hurt in the church today as they radically lower the number of addicted pastors over time.

The Distracted Pastor is constantly running around doing a million chores. There is hospital visitation, the church's finances, four committee meetings each week and maybe even a couple of board meetings for groups outside the church. Sermon preparation is limited by all this activity and the pastor can be testy and short with others because of overwork.

Worse, yet, when someone says, "Pastor, I really need to talk to you," the pastor responds by saying: "I have an opening in three weeks." When you are with the pastor it is clear that he or she wants the time together to end quickly because there is too much to do. We get annoyed when our dermatologist's office says they can't see us for eight weeks and we are worried if that thing on our neck is cancerous or not. We certainly don't want a pastor or pastoral staff that can't help us with a deep emotional crisis within a few days of our request. We'll see in a later chapter how devastating to a church a distracted pastor can be when it comes to weak sermon preparation.

Leaders of the laity, the ball is in your court if you have a distracted pastor. Go as a group, express your concern, and ask how the leadership can take tasks off the pastor's plate. Job descriptions for local church pastors have grown longer and longer over the last century. It is not biblical. The laity need to step up and be the Faithful Church. Pastors who refuse to delegate and allow the laity, discipled and trained, to be the backbone of the local church need to move on to new careers.

The Emotionally Fried Pastor has emerged in large numbers in the last forty years. Long job descriptions and gossipy, manipulative church members have taken their toll. Some pastors end up snappy or withdrawn. They may have reached the point where their marriage is impacted, and it is too weak to maintain the strains of professional ministry. A time of rest is desperately needed.

Regrettably, too many churches, movements and denominations no longer have the budgets to send emotionally fried pastors on three month trips to Europe as some did a century ago. Considering the tremendous emotional demands on pastors and the need for continuing

THE FEW, THE ROTTEN, THE DISTURBED PASTORS

education that involves more than a weekend conference, parts of these budgets need to be re-established. Pastors need to be able to rest early in the process of becoming emotionally fried.

My advice to anyone entering the ministry today who wishes to avoid the massive ranks of burned out pastors is two-fold:

1. Establish yourself in another profession before entering the ministry. With a bachelor's degree, a nine-month transition to teach course can gain you a public school teaching license in most states. For pastors with a master's degree it is even easier to get a teaching license. Somehow, someway, have a fallback employment position when a messed up church threatens your livelihood. Be able to take a one-year or more break from the ministry and not be financially devastated. Too many pastors remain in draining situations beyond the point of wisdom because of the lack of a backup career.

2. There are a lot of churches committed to American Civil Religion and they will not welcome your Kingdom-oriented vision. Consider using your second profession as a financial base for founding a brand new congregation that will be a Faithful Church from the beginning. The majority of large, healthy, faithful churches were founded in the last thirty years.

Pastors need to be cared for and encouraged. They need to be protected from gossips, manipulators and power brokers. Only then can the church be blessed with the best from their pastoral leadership.

Pastors also need to know where the boundaries are. They need to know exactly what happens when a pastor crosses one of those boundaries. It is not grace when a serial predator, mercenary, distracted or emotionally fried pastor is allowed to be a burden upon a church and its people.

Too many people get hurt for it possibly to be referred to as grace. Grace is a beautiful word, not an excuse for allowing destructive behavior to continue.

CHAPTER 7

Financial Transparency and Pastoral Accountability

I Corinthians 16: 3
Then, when I arrive, I will give letters of introduction to the men you approve and send them with your gift to Jerusalem.

The largest financial offering found in the New Testament is assuredly the Corinthian church's gift to the persecuted church in Jerusalem. Given the wealth found in the ancient city of Corinth and the passage above, the sum was probably quite high.

How did St. Paul want the money cared for? Did he say, "Put the money in a big bag and I'll carry it to Jerusalem for you?" No, he did not. He was a man of God. He never counted it himself, touched it with his own hands or determined which brothers and sisters in Jerusalem would receive it. He allowed the laity to care for the offering.

Did St. Paul say, "Give it to one man and he and I will travel to Jerusalem together?" No, he did not. In Greek, as in the English translation, the passage says that "men," in the plural, should take the money to Jerusalem. While the laity were caring for the funds, there was more than one of them. Today it is standard practice to use two people when we count offerings.

Did St. Paul say, "Let me choose the men who carry it to Jerusalem. I choose my cousin, my best friend and a person who has never dared to disagree with one of my ministry decisions." No, he did not. He was a man of God. He wanted the Corinthian congregation to choose people they approved of to care for the money as it made its way to Jerusalem. In one simple verse St. Paul gives us a model for taking care of an offering.

> Then, when I arrive, I will give letters of introduction to the *men you approve* and send *them* with your gift to Jerusalem. (I Cor. 16:3)

Paul was a tent-making missionary who was more often than not making his own living as he founded a church in a new city. When a new church grew to the point where all of his time was needed for the ministry, he would finally accept a salary. Then he would train up leaders, hand the church over to them and head to another city to found another church. During its founding he would be a tent-maker again. He regularly left salaried ministry positions to become a tent-making church founder! He was obviously not in the ministry for the salary, the power to disburse funds as he pleased, the benefits or the security.

Paul understood that a congregation needs to trust its spiritual leaders. Without a transparent and laity-driven financial system people get hurt. Financial excess, out-of-control spending on questionable projects, embezzlement, luxurious hotels for continuing education events with liquor from the pricey hotel bar, mileage reimbursements beyond anything reasonable and a general sense of secrecy about church finances leave laypeople with a sense of hurt that their spiritual leader could function in these ways. They leave churches, and some, unbiblically, vow never to return to an organized church.

Meanwhile, many pastors will legitimately gripe about their congregation's low giving. Most dying congregations give between two to three percent of their income to the church instead of their full tithe. If the people did give more, there would be resources to invest in growth-oriented ministries such as high-quality youth and children's programs.

What too many well-intentioned pastors don't understand are the basics for establishing a trust relationship with the congregation regarding finances. Having spent half my adult life as a pastor and half as a layperson I've seen that:

- Laypeople want to feel that when they give to God, the money will be controlled by the laity, used wisely, and transparently reported with monthly or quarterly financial reports that can be easily understood. An annual audit of some sort is appreciated by most and builds trust.

- The laity want to understand the vision of the church and how their tithes and offerings are going toward building the Kingdom of God. Vision casting connected to the release of the next year's budget is crucial.

- Laypeople do not object to solid, biblical teaching from Jesus' words in the Gospels about giving and being financially committed to the Kingdom. They respect a pastor who is not afraid to teach what Jesus taught. It is part of discipleship, and anyone who would flee a congregation because of biblical teachings about giving are people who are not interested in building the Kingdom, anyway. We'll pray for them, but not agonize over their departure or allow their threat of leaving to keep the full Gospel from being taught. The strong majority appreciates teaching from the Scriptures.

- Emergency appeals in order to pay the bills, meet the budget and replace the roof will often cause a congregation to step up and meet that need. Long-term it will cause the same congregation to question the wisdom of whoever is at the financial helm. Why is the budget so out of whack with the church's income? Why was the budget raised so radically last year? Why weren't reserves set aside little by little for the last ten years when everyone knew how old the roof was? Emergency appeals damage trust. They should be for true emergencies and should be done apologetically by whoever is responsible for the mistake that was made. Using them regularly and routinely is a good way to rid the congregation of intelligent people who don't wish to be manipulated.

Nothing in this chapter should be understood as a justification for not giving one's tithe. If we do not trust our local church body to transparently care for our tithe we need to move to another church or give our tithe to a nonprofit Christian mission agency until we do feel comfortable giving to our local church.

Many pastors will not like the last paragraph, and I can envision this book sailing across the room when they read it. Pastors, here's the reality: If your church's finances are not transparent and connected to a well-explained vision, then you are not doing what you need to do to gain the congregation's trust.

Storehouse tithing, the concept that the tithe or ten percent should be given to the house where one is spiritually fed, is justifiable. But, if there is no financial transparency, if there is darkness and a lack of light, if funds are being spent irresponsibly, then the laity are justified in not supporting darkness and sending part or all of their tithe to a local homeless shelter or an overseas mission agency.

All Christians have a responsibility to give their tithe to the Lord. We are also called to give our offerings, as well, based upon how financially blessed we are. No layperson or clergy is allowed to steal from the Lord (Malachi 3:8-12). If we don't trust our church's financial leadership, we need to speak up and encourage change.

Here's a good understanding of financial transparency. Check off the box if you believe the practices below would build trust. Circle the box if it is actually occurring in your church.

- ☐ The paid staff and pastors are not involved in counting or depositing the offering.

- ☐ At least two laypeople are with the offering until it is locked into an unopenable deposit bag or carried to the bank.

- ☐ If a pastor is one of the signatories on church checks, then he or she is not the only signatory required on the check. Church credit cards are used only for appropriate expenses, and two members of the laity each month check them, along with the receipts. Paid bookkeepers that are hired and fired by the pastor do not fulfill this responsibility.

- ☐ If the church is larger than twenty people, the pastor's relatives are in no way involved in the financial life of the church.

- ☐ The pastor's complete compensation is decided by a group of laity that includes none of his or her relatives. The pastor is allowed input, but then leaves the room before the final discussion and decision is made. Once decided, the entire compensation package is distributed to the congregation on paper or through the web in an obvious and known place.

Some mainline denominations require the publication of the pastors' salaries to the membership, but some local churches have developed the habit of releasing the pastor's salary without mentioning the fair rental value of the parsonage, utilities paid by the church, the cost of health insurance and retirement paid by the church, continuing education costs (including luxurious hotels), cell phone and mileage reimbursements, etc. The failure to disclose any part of the pastor's compensation package is scurrilous and is not walking in the light. Moreover, it damages trust when discovered.

- ☐ Monthly or Quarterly financial statements are made available to the congregation. These financial statements should be easy to understand and not presented in such a way that only an accountant can understand them.

- ☐ An audit of the church's finances should be done at the end of each year. If a congregation is small and does not wish to pay for this service, then a sister or brother from another congregation may be asked to come in to look at the financial practices and examine every fifth transaction. A letter is then written from this objective viewpoint and presented to the congregation or placed on the web. If changes are recommended then the layperson in charge of the finances may write a response letter disagreeing or promising to make the necessary changes for the next year.

- ☐ Once a year, a financial report and a proposed budget, in line with the vision of the church, are presented to the congregation.

Again, check the boxes that you agree would build trust between a congregation and its leadership. Circle those that are taking place in the congregation that you consider to be your spiritual home.

Pastoral Accountability

Trust is increased between a pastor and the congregation when the people know the pastor is accountable to someone. It may be a District Superintendent, an elder's board or a fellow pastor.

Laity know they are accountable to their pastor. If they have a question or are struggling in their marriage, they have a pastor they can go to. Who can pastors turn to in similar situations? Who's keeping the clergy on track? If pastors can avoid certain pitfalls, fewer people will be hurt or become disillusioned in the congregation.

Here are a few accountability questions that great pastors allow themselves to be asked at least once a month. Great pastors seek out those who will be bold enough to ask questions like:

FINANCIAL TRANSPARENCY AND PASTORAL ACCOUNTABILITY

- How's your marriage? Is there anything in your life that might harm your marriage? Have you taken your wife on a date recently?

- Are you finding sufficient time for teaching and sermon preparation?

- Are you actively selecting and training up leaders in your congregation. Specifically, what have you done this month for leadership development?

- Are you actively involved in discipling new Christians or in overseeing a discipleship process? Are your sheep growing in the Lord?

- Is there anything in your finances for which you need to repent?

- How are your spiritual disciplines? Are you reading Scripture, fasting, praying and worshipping occasionally in a setting where you are not leading worship? What other spiritual disciplines, such as listening to sermons from great preachers or enjoying praise music while you drive, have you actively engaged in this month?

- What is the weakest portion of your ministry, personally speaking? What continuing education events will you attend this year, or what mentoring relationships will you enter in order to strengthen this area?

- Are you respecting a Sabbath day each week? Sunday is not a day off for you but are you taking another day as your Sabbath?

- Are you engaging in retreats once a month so that you can hear from God and bring vision to the church?

- How are you leading your congregation to reach the community for Christ? How are you leading your congregation to meet the needs of the community?

As mainline denominations have closed churches by the thousands and lost members by the millions, budgets for district offices have shrunk precipitously. Many have transitioned from one superintendent overseeing forty churches to one superintendent overseeing eighty churches to save money.

The result is less accountability for each pastor. Most mainline pastors fill out yearly written reports. Most are convinced no one ever has time to read them. Accountability has devolved to the point where pastors are only held accountable if their church does not pay its portion of the district budget. Simply because a denomination or movement has a hierarchy does not mean it engages in spiritual or ministry accountability.

Great pastors find a group of fellow pastors to meet with in person or by group video chat at least once a month. These relationships deepen by the decade as pastors ask each other hard questions like the ones listed above.

FINANCIAL TRANSPARENCY AND PASTORAL ACCOUNTABILITY

The discussions in these groups shape a pastor and occasionally work their way into sermons. The laity hear that their pastor is accountable to someone. It engenders trust and results in far fewer people getting hurt.

CHAPTER 8

Difficulty Breaking Into Social Groups

Leviticus 19:34-35
The alien living with you must be treated as one of your native-born. Love him as yourself, for you were aliens in Egypt, I am the Lord your God.

One of the best ways to be a church that hurts others is to have someone attend your worship service week after week and make them feel shunned instead of welcomed. Loneliness in a place that is supposed to be welcoming produces its own kind of hurt.

When our family is on vacation we visit other churches of various sizes. Most of the time we come in, sit down, worship, stand up and leave without another living soul speaking to us. Before worship there are a dozen groups of people talking and laughing and enjoying each other's fellowship. It is the same after the worship ends. And then there is our family, awkwardly sitting in full view of everyone with no recognition we are alive.

A true theology of hospitality, which includes speaking to another person, has become lost in congregations that have rigidly closed social groups. New attendees can come into a congregation and be there for months. No pastoral visits are made and no one invites them to lunch.

They hear about that exciting mission trip to Haiti but no one personally invites them. They decide not to call the leader of the mission trip because they would be going on the trip with complete strangers. Worse yet, who wants to go on a mission trip with people who have been ignoring you month after month! The same sense of estrangement keeps the person from coming to the church-wide yard sale or any other activity.

Some local congregations recruit members of the congregation to be greeters. In this way a visitor at least gets one guaranteed handshake at the door. Wiser congregations train and seed the back portion of the worship area, where visitors tend to sit, with extroverts who intentionally look for people they don't know and who don't seem to be talking to anyone before or after the service.

Use Me or Lose Me

I thought it was the coolest thing I had seen in a long time. While in a church new to our family there was a stapled packet in the lobby with four sheets that we couldn't miss as we walked into the worship area. "Serving Opportunities," it said in big print. I opened it and walked into the sanctuary where no one spoke to us for the fourth Sunday in a row.

DIFFICULTY BREAKING INTO SOCIAL GROUPS

The packet was filled with the opportunities for service in this congregation of 900 per weekend. The children's ministry covered the first page with twenty-two possibilities! Teachers and sound technicians and check-in people were needed. The backside had twelve youth-related and five adult ministry opportunities. There was another page with worship and outreach people needed. We could help garden a section of the church grounds with the fresh produce going to a homeless shelter. We could help with jail ministry or be on the kitchen or library team. What a great idea! I recommend one of these packets for every congregation to help new people get involved!

As the spiritual leader of the home I filled mine out, then sat down with each member of the family to help fill theirs out. Service to the church and the community is a family value. What an incredible idea this packet is! It invited us into service and invited us to form friendships within our new congregation. The back page told me to turn the sheets into the church office once they were filled out. I did and waited for my family to be invited into service.

And we waited. And we waited. Finally, one ministry from page five on my sheet called and invited me to do repair projects with them in underprivileged people's homes. I've enjoyed working with those guys one Saturday a month. There was one phone call from seventeen combined boxes my family checked on our individual sheets.

Ten weeks after we turned in the sheets, one of the pastors preached on how the church is incomplete without each one of us being involved. He mentioned the fact that twenty percent of the congregation does eighty percent of the work, and that the congregation needs to be more involved. We all have spiritual gifts and need to use them.

While I agreed with every point in his sermon, I almost raised my hand in the middle of it to share our experience with the Serving Opportunities packet! My emotions ranged from frustration to sadness to a bit of anger. I emailed the pastor two days later. He wrote back, apologized, and asked us to re-submit the Serving Opportunities packets. We did and have not heard back.

In case you are wondering, my family has the same skin color as the majority of this congregation. We dress like they do and we seem to be of the same socio-economic group. All of us use deodorant and mouthwash. These are not legitimate reasons, but they were not the reasons in our case. We suffer from one disease. We are new.

A congregation that truly values new people will put the responsibility for inclusion on the existing congregation and the church leadership, not on the visitor. If someone visits more than three times, isn't it time to send a person into their living room to help them fill out the Serving Opportunities packet or just to get to know them? Then the person connects them with each ministry leader and keeps checking back until the ministry leaders have connected with the new people. The responsibility is on the congregation to be hospitable, not the new person to somehow force their way in. By the way, our family attends a different church now.

DIFFICULTY BREAKING INTO SOCIAL GROUPS

The church is a series of concentric circles. On the outer ring is the first-time visitor. On the inner circle is the most active and committed of laypersons in the congregation.

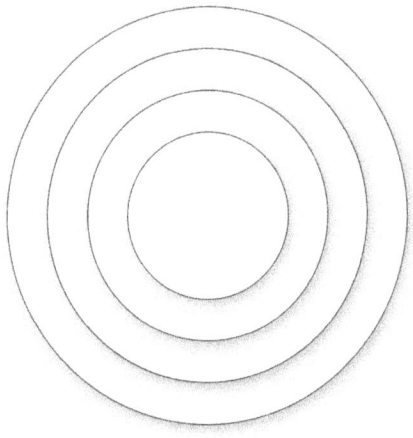

The ever-present job of the congregation and the leaders is to invite people on the outside rings to come one ring closer to the center. Within service we find relationship and connection to the Body of Christ.

Lay people can leave a congregation feeling hurt if their spiritual gifts are not discovered, developed and used. Of course some are resistant to give their time to the work of the Lord. Others, many others, are waiting to be asked. If they are not asked they will be checking out new churches within a few months. If that doesn't work, they may give up on the Body of Christ because its walls are too steep and hard to climb over.

Questions for Reflection

What could you *personally* do to make visitors and new attendees feel more welcomed and included in your church?

_____
_____
_____
_____

What could your congregation do to make visitors and new attendees feel more welcomed and included in your church?

_____
_____
_____
_____

CHAPTER 9

Struggling and Failing At Small Groups

I Corinthians 12: 12-13
Just as a body, though one, has many parts, but all its many parts form one body, so it is with Christ. For we were all baptized by one Spirit so as to form one body—whether Jews or Gentiles, slave or free—and we were all given the one Spirit to drink.

Jesse was lonely. After the divorce he ended up with custody of all three boys, and his days were jam-packed. With work at the factory in the Mid-West and taking care of the kids, his schedule was full during the week. He tried to be in the art community of his small city when his wife had custody of the boys two weekends a month. He loved painting, but he still felt a need for a healthier group of friends.

That's when Jesse brought the boys to a Wednesday night youth program where he could join one of the adult

Bible studies at the same time as their program. He truly connected after that, attending worship regularly, painting murals on the church's interior walls, and tithing. He was a small group success story from every angle. His loneliness went away and he felt a renewed sense of purpose to his life. He grew in his knowledge of the Scriptures and in discipleship.

Our society has become extremely lonely. A large number of people are looking to have their relational needs met when they come to visit a church. They may stay for a while because of the music and the preaching, but if that need for a new and healthy friendship base is not met they will grow to be uncomfortable and hurt. They may say, 'That church didn't meet my needs. Maybe no church ever will.' Without a healthy small group program, most new people simply do not anchor into a church.

I train pastors part-time and do occasional consulting work. I have asked over eighty active pastors what their experience is with small groups. Their responses fall into three categories:

1. Our small groups are healthy, vibrant and the primary driver of our growth, both in numbers, in discipleship training and in increasing the people's depth of Christian commitment.

2. We tried. We really tried. Our people did not want to sign up and attend and we gave up. Small groups work for some churches but not for ours.

3. I'm tired of hearing about small groups. We have them and they have added nothing to our growth in Christian depth or numbers.

After I saw these three categories clearly, I started asking a lot more questions about how leaders were implementing small groups. What made it work in some places and not in others? Was it the particular culture around the church? Was it providing or not providing food? Was small group leader training a factor? Here's the results of talking to these pastors:

A. The training of small group leaders is the primary difference between the successful small groups mentioned in category #1 versus those in categories #2 and #3. Successful small group systems in local churches have carefully selected and trained group leaders. Someone high up in the church's teaching leadership, usually the lead pastor, has put together a well-thought-through program for selecting, training and mentoring small group leaders. Meanwhile, churches that were unhappy with the results of their efforts with small groups almost never had a selection and training program for leaders.

B. The majority of churches with successful small group systems had direct input from the lead pastor. He or she led a group. They trained leaders. They strategized, strengthened and were constantly involved in making the groups better and better. Their sermons included illustrations from those whose lives had been transformed within the small groups. In other words, the lead pastor lived and breathed small groups. It was never intended to be a secondary program in the church. *In the lead pastor's mind, it is the life blood of the church.* If there was an organizational chart, the small groups were the center circle, and the largest circle, of all the ministries in the church.

Meanwhile, pastors from groups #2 and #3 saw small groups as one of many programs in the life of the church. Often a staff member was tasked with caring for the small group program with a portion of their time. The lead pastor had almost no direct oversight or training role in the program. If there is a woman's program, a children's program and a small group program, all of their circles would be the same size on the chart.

C. Because small group leader training was never done, the pastors of churches #2 and #3 never communicated to group leaders the expectation that group members were to invite friends, grow, disciple, pastorally care for most of the member's needs and mentor new leaders. Eventually the goal is to divide into two healthy, growing groups that eventually became four, then eight, then sixteen groups. This vision may exist in the pastor's mind, but was never effectively communicated to the group leaders. Vision for the small group system was not passed on from one level of leadership to the next.

D. The group member's relational needs have to be met. Food, a time for relaxed fellowship and a time when the passage studied became applicable to group member's lives is critical. Somehow people open up and become relational when a bit of food is served and the agenda for the evening is paused. People want to just chat and have their relational needs met. Modern people are terribly lonely.

Training group leaders to ask open-ended questions about what the Bible passage means for their lives allows group members to be the ones who apply the text to their lives. The time goes from surface level chatting over food to a deeper level of sharing hurts, successes and personal struggles as the Word of God is applied to people's lives. Again, emotional and relational needs get met.

E. Group members in successful small group systems experienced God. God was experienced in the Bible study and in the application time. Other group members spoke the Word of God into each other's lives. God's voice was heard. We not only carry within us a need to be in relationship with other people, we also carry a need to be in relationship with the Creator of the Universe. It is built into the very fiber of our being.

Small group systems that focus on riding roller coasters together or fixing their cars together or making crafts have a much lower rate of success unless there is a component where people experience God in the midst of it.

A lead pastor needs to have clearly in his mind what he wants the small group system to accomplish. Is it:

- Numerical growth?

- Depth of biblical knowledge?

- Discipleship?

- People being pastored and cared for?

What are the goals and how will the lead pastor make sure these goals are met?

Wrapping It Up

If the lead pastor does not value discipleship and teaching the Word of God, a small group system in his or her church will never work well. Even if groups meet, they will add relatively little to the life of the church. If the lead pastor sets goals for the small group ministry, promotes them, lifts them up as a high value, helps design and helps to evaluate and re-create it each year, small groups can flourish. They can transform a church.

It is difficult to track down who first said, "As goes the pulpit, so goes the church," but it is exceedingly true. If the lead pastor wants a healthy small group system that disciples, deepens and grows the church, it will happen. It will happen even without the initial support of the laity. It will happen even if it begins with one group meeting in the pastor's living room and grows from there until finally the resistant laity embrace it because of the good it does.

The call for pastors to be the First Teachers of the local church is a biblical call. If Jesus is our model for ministry, then how should we be ministering? Jesus taught. For three years he taught! Even after the resurrection he appeared to two disciples and "explained to them the things concerning Himself in all the Scriptures" (Luke 24:27). The Apostles were so focused on teaching after Pentecost that when the ministry became complicated by other matters they appointed deacons because, "It would not be right for us to neglect the ministry of the Word of God in order to wait on tables" (Acts 6: 2).

As the spiritual descendants of Jesus Christ and of the Apostles, pastors are the First Teachers in the church and need to be integrally involved in the development and life of the church's small group ministry.

Sometimes the phrase, "I was hurt by a local church," really translates as, "My needs were not met so I left." Healthy small groups have the potential to help churches meet those needs. What it will require, though, is a new commitment by many lead pastors to disciple making and a return to what St. Paul considers a pastor's job to be:

> "To equip his people for works of service, so that the body of Christ may be built up until we all reach unity in the faith and in the knowledge of

the Son of God and become mature, attaining to the whole measure of the fullness of Christ. Then we will no longer be infants, tossed back and forth by the waves, and blown here and there by every wind of teaching and by the cunning and craftiness of people in their deceitful scheming. Instead, speaking the truth in love, we will grow to become in every respect the mature body of him who is the head, that is, Christ. From him the whole body, joined and held together by every supporting ligament, grows and builds itself up in love, as each part does its work" (Ephesians 4: 12-16).

If you are looking for a training resource for small groups leaders or to increase your own understanding of healthy small groups, consider Joel Comiskey's, *How to Lead a Great Cell Group Meeting… So People Want to Come Back*, 2011.

If your church does not offer a small group system that includes numerical growth, biblical knowledge, discipleship and application of the Word for today with a trained leader who knows how to lead one of these groups, please find one outside your local church. Two nation-wide organizations that are theologically and biblically sound are Community Bible Study and Bible Study Fellowship. Their groups meet in most communities.

http://www.communitybiblestudy.org
https://www.bsfinternational.org

CHAPTER 10

You Have a Pulse? You Can Be a Member.

Ephesians 4:14
Then we will no longer be infants, tossed back and forth by the waves, and blown here and there by every wind of teaching.

A man named Dave walked into a small church on Sunday in Tampa, Florida, five years ago. He smelled bad. His clothes and hair were rumpled. He never put together a full sentence that morning. Half the congregation avoided him and was obviously uncomfortable. The other half had heard enough of the Gospel that they greeted this homeless man warmly.

Dave came to the church office the next day and we talked. He thanked me because two of the church members had taken him to lunch and then shopping for clothes. These two guys then drove him to his camp in the woods behind the grocery store to get his old, dirty clothes. The Laundromat was the next stop, and then the grocery store.

Dave was talking in full sentences on Monday morning. We talked for two hours about what had led him to homelessness and it was clear that his inability to function in society had a lot to do with hunger and the trials of living in the woods. Mosquitoes had bitten him everywhere. My wife and I felt led to 'lend' him a camping tent when he didn't want to go to a shelter. We doubted we would see it again, and it ended up burning to the ground two months later due to another homeless person lighting it on fire. A fund the congregation had set up bought him a pre-paid cell phone.

Dave was employed three days later because he had clothes, food, shelter and a way for the employer to call him. Not all homeless men have a deep desire to come out of their situation and respond so well. Dave did, and the church rejoiced.

For the months that Dave was in the church, before he moved to another city where he had relatives, he said a lot of hurtful things to the people of the congregation. Often his mouth started moving before his brain engaged. Dave still had a bunch of issues to resolve in his life.

No one minded. There was a not a single person in the congregation who left the church angry because of what he said to them. If I had said even one of the things he said, the person would be offended, hurt, angry and thinking about leaving the congregation and never coming back.

Dave taught me something of great value. A Christian congregation is a bathtub. When dirty people come in to get cleaned up the congregation is not easily offended by the dirty person. They keep loving him or her and wiping the dirt off.

YOU HAVE A PULSE? YOU CAN BE A MEMBER.

Make that person a member or a leader or a paid staff person and suddenly people get offended, hurt and angry because "the church" has hurt them. People don't leave congregations because of what attenders or visitors say to them.

After forty years of being a part of all sorts of congregations in three countries, I have never seen someone leave a congregation due to hurt or anger because of what an attender said or did to them. It has only been members, leaders, staff and pastors that cause people to get hurt even though attenders say plenty of hurtful, stupid things, as well.

Sometimes the lessons the homeless teach us are the most valuable ones.

I never thought about asking Dave to become a member. I made sure he got connected to a church where he was going when he moved to another state, but it never occurred to me to bring him into membership, even after he accepted Christ and decided, all on his own, to start tithing. He wasn't ready. There were still moral and mental health issues that made membership a bad idea. I pray that he is a solid member of a congregation today, and I pray he was healed enough to not hurt people.

In most denominations, traditions and independent congregations, membership means that the person has the right and responsibility to help set the direction of the church. Even staff-led congregations bring to the membership big decisions such as building a new building. Everyone votes and the members have helped to set the future direction of the congregation. In others, the membership elects the board or elders once a year and then those elders decide who will be the pastor, what the budget will be, and a host of other decisions. The reality is that bringing someone into membership too quickly, before they are biblically knowledgeable and spiritually mature, affects the future of the congregation.

It means the future direction of the church may not be what God wants it to be because there is a member, with a persuasive voice and vote, who is unable to hear or acknowledge God's voice. Add a hundred spiritually immature voices to the membership and the future of the congregation could be bleak indeed. Toss in a number of gossips, manipulators and power brokers with a voice and a vote and the church is doomed.

More importantly, membership gives official status. It means someone represents the church. If they go and say something hurtful then the congregation takes a small public relations hit. If a hundred members say something hurtful and spiritually immature once a month, then the congregation develops a truly bad reputation. In the community, a congregation is known by its members. In marketing terms, our brand is determined by the spiritual maturity of our membership.

In the Last Thirty Years...

In the name of a theology of hospitality, a key Old Testament concept, many churches have opened their membership rolls to anyone who can breathe. 'The more members the bigger we are! Come one, come all! The church has open doors! Are you an assassin for the mafia? Come on in! The first Sunday of every month is for new members. Just

YOU HAVE A PULSE? YOU CAN BE A MEMBER.

come forward when the pastor says it is time. Please don't shoot anyone while you are in the church, but… Welcome! We believe in hospitality.' An Old Testament message that insured food and a place to rest has been misinterpreted to mean membership.

Our bar has fallen so low in membership within the United States that a relatively high bar for membership involves four evening sessions of an hour each and a short meeting with a member of the staff. Is that enough to assure that a person or couple is biblically knowledgeable and spiritually mature? Can we even be sure they are not addicted to gossip and manipulation with this level of carelessness? Considering that each potential member is coming from a thoroughly messed up culture, we should be terrified to accept just anyone. Only knowing them very well should bring about an invitation to membership.

If a hundred people join the church tomorrow, simply because they have a pulse, your regional superintendent may be happy. The problem is that statistically the pastor just brought in five of the hundred people who are committed to gossip and manipulation, and the pastor will pay a high price for it sooner or later. These are people who run their Facebook page like an eighth grader. The congregation will pay a price for bringing them into membership.

In addition to a non-biblical understanding of hospitality, the church in this country has lowered its bar for membership because of universalism. It is a big word but it is easy to understand.

Universalism is the heretical belief that everyone is going to heaven. Those with faith in Jesus, those without faith,

Buddhists, Muslims, and unrepentant assassins for the mafia are all going to heaven. This theology is based on God being a loving God who could never, ever keep someone out of heaven. Universalism says that if they are going to heaven anyway, then everyone should be brought into membership in the church with no pre-conditions like knowing how to pray. It fails to take into account passages in the Bible where God is shown to be loving but also to be a God who judges.[26]

True biblical theology, taught by the Faithful Church for two thousand years, recognizes that God will not force someone to be in heaven for eternity who has rejected Him all of their life on earth. God doesn't force us into heaven.

In John 14:6 Jesus says, "I am the way and the truth and the life. No one comes to the Father except through me." It is not poetry. It is not a parable. We should read this text in the straightforward manner in which it was intended. It is in agreement with the other three Gospels and every New Testament writer. Belief and walking with Jesus is the only way to experience the abundant life here on earth and eternal life. Jesus is *the* way.

Today parts of the church have rejected this teaching and have embraced an open door policy that sounds good to our tolerant culture. The problem is that it is not faithful to the original intent of the biblical authors.

Universalism is certainly taught in the Unitarian Universalist movement. All are welcome. There are absolutely no membership requirements. A Buddhist, an agnostic, an atheist and a heretical Christian can all join in fellowship

---

[26] Acts 5:1-11. This is a reference to the Ananias and Sapphira story.

YOU HAVE A PULSE? YOU CAN BE A MEMBER.

together and study each other's ideas on how to live a happy life. I'm sure they have a good time together, but it is not the Faithful Church based on the Old and New Testaments.

The final reason the church in the U.S. has lowered its requirements for membership is the never-ending search for numbers. When pastors are judged by the number of new members brought in, and only on that number, then the pressures are in the direction of a low bar for membership.

Potential members could be secretly struggling with addiction or have beaten up their child the night before they become members. As long as no one knows their deep, dark secrets or the level of their biblical illiteracy, receiving them as members is risky. They could be terrible gossips and manipulators, and all some churches care about is increasing the overall number of members.

Our collective theology of membership has become so low in the last sixty years in the Protestant church that one wonders if a theology regarding membership even exists any more in many churches.

We had 134¾ In Church on Sunday

As a missionary in the Far East of Russia twenty years ago, I asked a Russian Orthodox bishop, what they call the pastor of a local congregation, how large his congregation was. He answered that last Sunday he had 134¾ in church and that was the number he sent in to the Patriarch's office in Moscow for the official report.

All sorts of thoughts went through my head about how you get ¾ of a person in church. He finally finished speaking and I asked how he came to that number. After going around and around a few times we finally found our cultural difference. We count the number of people assuming that each one present counts for 1.

He was counting by one-quarters. If he saw a woman in the worship service who never came during the week, only attended twice a month and showed no signs of Christian maturity, he wrote down "¼" on his sheet. If there was a fully committed Christian in attendance who was active in service to the community and spiritually mature, only then would he write a "1." The fractions "½" and "¾" were involved for others of limited commitment to Christ.

I attended his worship service the next Sunday. It was over three hours long and there were no chairs or pews. We stood. For one full hour of the service the Bishop was standing on a raised platform taking attendance while an assistant led the liturgy. I counted about 250 by my North American counting method. After the service, with aching feet and a hurting back from standing on tile for three hours, and my head slightly woozy from the incense, I asked him how many were in worship. He smiled and said "140½."

He showed me his paperwork from that hour of taking attendance. It had three columns. The first was for the person's name. He knew the names of his sheep. The second was the count, ¼, ½, ¾, or 1. The third column was what he and his leaders needed to do during the upcoming week to see that a particular person increased their number until they were a full 1. The third column was his and his staff's to do list for the next week.

YOU HAVE A PULSE? YOU CAN BE A MEMBER.

After making a copy, this was the document he sent to his superiors in Moscow. That man was a pastor with a growing congregation. The ½'s were becoming ¾'s. The ¾'s were becoming 1's. The leaders in Moscow did hold him accountable for growth, but it was growth connected to spiritual depth, not just warm bodies.

The Russian Orthodox Church has a multitude of issues it is facing. Counting spiritually immature attendees like we do in the United States is not one of them. In the West, we need to learn how to count.

A Healthy Fear

Fear can be a good motivator for changing our behavior. Here is a healthy and beautiful fear for every Christian leader:

Consider your flock. If you are a small group leader, then it is those who attend your small group. If you are the director of the Children's program, then it is all of the children and the teachers you oversee.

Now comes the scary question: One day you will walk through the gates of heaven and enter by the grace of God. Now look over your shoulder. How many of your flock will be behind you and actually entering heaven?

If there are less than 100% then there is a list you need to make with three columns this week. It is the Russian Bishop's list. The third column, how to get each to grow, is half of your job description as a Christian leader. The other half is outreach. But if, like so many "growing" churches, we are only concerned about outreach and increasing numbers, then we are missing the mark regarding the biblical call to raise up disciples.

Outreach is great! Reaching the community for Christ is fantastic! But if ¼'s stay ¼'s for year after year, and we never do anything about it, then we are not living under this very healthy fear for a Christian leader.

Will your flock follow you into heaven?

Meanwhile...

While the majority of churches have no intentional discipleship program and an open door to membership for anyone, people are getting hurt in the church. With a bunch of ¼'s running around who are full members of the church, representing the church to the community and hurting people whenever they wish, people keep leaving the church and vowing never to return. The public gives our brand dismal ratings.

This church in Indiana is advertising for nothing more than Pew Fillers. Taken 9-30-2015.

YOU HAVE A PULSE? YOU CAN BE A MEMBER.

I love the question, "If Jesus is our model for ministry then how should we be ministering?" Let's get real. If Jesus had formed a local congregation, would he have allowed the hard core Pharisees to join the membership? No! He would have called them a brood of vipers and chased them out as He did in Matthew 23:33.

If Jesus had known that an active pedophile or a not-yet-healed arsonist or a unrepentant serial killer wanted to be a member, he would have loved the church enough to say, "Not Yet!" He would have met with them, offered healing, and only once they exhibited Christian maturity would he have moved them from attenders to members. The same goes for destructive gossips and others who hurt people regularly and freely.

A few years back I was a member of a Rotary Club in Tampa, Florida.

Expectations were expressed clearly before they accepted me into membership. Your dues are $342/quarter, they told me. You will be in service to the community twice a quarter. You will attend 50 of 52 meetings each year. If you do not fulfill any of these requirements you will be given three months to come into compliance. If you do not, your membership will be revoked. After I turned in my application for membership, along with a letter of reference from a member who vouched for my integrity, three members of the board sat down with me. I was interviewed and expectations were very clearly laid out.

The Four Way Test was explained to me. It is like Scripture for Rotarians. If a member's business practices come in conflict with the Four Way Test, then membership will be removed.

I was told of Rotary's commitment to end polio. It is now 99% eradicated in the world. I was told that I was expected to give personally and help raise money for this cause above and beyond my quarterly dues. Then I was asked if I still wanted to join. I happily joined the membership because there was a sense of purpose and direction to being a member.

The next week I mentioned to my pastor that I wanted to join the church as a member. Four days later, with no preparation, I was in front of the congregation and I was in. The difference between the two memberships was quite stark. One had expectations and the other did not. This church grew so weak over the next five years from people getting hurt and leaving that the few dozen remaining members were folded into a new church start and their old church ceased to exist.

If membership is open to anyone, including gossips, troublemakers, the apathetic and the emotionally troubled, it is no wonder people get hurt in church. Often there are no boundaries placed on behavior once a person enters membership and there were no boundaries for entering membership, either. The members, who represent the church to the community, help to give the church a very bad name.

Who Do We Judge?

I can hear the objections already. The church is not to be a place of judgments! We already have a bad reputation in

YOU HAVE A PULSE? YOU CAN BE A MEMBER.

the world as being pharisaical and shaking our fingers at others! Who am I to judge! The nice version of Jesus I have in my head was not judgmental!

Ephesians chapter 5 is the response to these objections. St. Paul agrees that we are not to judge those who are in the world. If someone has not come into fellowship, we are absolutely *not* to judge the person (verses 9-10). It is only those who have come into fellowship who are to be judged (Verses 1-2, 4-5, 9, 11-13).

I Corinthians 5:12-13 sums it up beautifully:

> What business is it of mine to judge those outside the church? Are you not to judge those inside? God will judge those outside. "Expel the wicked man from among you."[27]

This is very much the approach that Jesus took with his judgments. For the Samaritan woman at the well there was no judgment in his words. She was not in fellowship with the Jews and he wanted her to be in fellowship.

Meanwhile, when Jesus spoke to the majority of the Pharisees, he called them a brood of vipers (and a host of other names)! He reserved his judgments for those inside the fellowship of the Jews, and especially those who were in leadership but were not following God. His judgment for those inside was strong and harsh. He was not judgmental to those outside. This is the biblical Jesus.

---

[27] Paul is quoting from Deuteronomy 17:7.

Questions for Reflection

Maria and Patrick want to become members of your congregation. Which parts of their spiritual maturity need to be in place and solid before you, personally, would want them to become members? What is your theology of membership?

_____
_____
_____
_____

What tools would you use to help them reach this level of spiritual maturity? Some of the possibilities include:

- Small groups

- Time with a leading member of the congregation

- Bible study classes

- A class on the Apostles' Creed

- One-on-one mentoring regarding any addictions and habits

- A certain number of months of tithing

- Proven service to the community

- Evangelism training

YOU HAVE A PULSE? YOU CAN BE A MEMBER.

- A conversation about the church's covenant together and internal discipline (living together outside marriage, adultery and other ethical issues). How would you help people reach the maturity level needed to meet the theology of membership you expressed in the last question?

_____
_____
_____
_____
_____
_____
_____
_____
_____
_____
_____
_____

As you develop a sound theology of membership you are declaring yourself to be a part of the Faithful Church.

CHAPTER 11

Pain Because the Scriptures Are Not Taught

II Timothy 4:3
For the time will come when people will not put up with sound doctrine. Instead, to suit their own desires, they will gather around them a great number of teachers to say what their itching ears want to hear.

The 50-year old pastor was crying like a baby. Weeping may be the better word. He had kept his emotions bottled up inside in order to seem professional, and finally the dam had burst. I put my arm around him and let him weep. When the wave of emotion had run its course I asked him to tell me the story of how the church had hurt him. Here is the story:

Dwayne had arrived at a downtown church just a year earlier. The city was a port on the Mid-Atlantic Coast. The pastor serving before Dwayne had done no intentional discipleship and no intentional leadership development for a decade. If someone was a captain of industry, wealthy, or came from a prestigious family in this old city, the previous pastor invited them into leadership. Biblical knowledge or spiritual maturity was of no importance.

Dwayne arrived and began preaching in Genesis. Then he moved into Exodus. His pastoral oversight committee was furious. They felt sermons should only be from the New Testament because it is more gentle and filled with grace. They never actually said anything to Dwayne, though, and just sat on their strong feelings.

In this denomination, the pastoral oversight committee is the group that relates to the district superintendent (DS) and recommends each year if the pastor should stay or go. The chairperson of the committee called the DS and asked for an emergency meeting four days later. Only when the DS was there did they finally share their feelings about the Old Testament having no place in their church.

Faced with a unanimous committee the DS tried to bring healthy theology into the room, but it didn't seem to be working. In order to compromise with this powerful committee, the pastor spoke up and offered to leave the book of Exodus – for now – and begin preaching from a New Testament book. He felt a little give and take in the midst of a room filled with emotion was the path of wisdom.

On Sunday the pastor preached. After the first two minutes of the sermon he noticed the chairperson of the committee stand and exit. Other members of the committee followed him out.

Once outside the sanctuary they called the DS and implored him to come to the church right away. He was

PAIN BECAUSE THE SCRIPTURES ARE NOT TAUGHT

with his family at another church and begged off. The chairperson threatened to move every belonging of the pastor's onto the lawn of the parsonage unless the DS came immediately. The DS gave in, arranging for someone else to take his family home after worship.

An hour later the DS walked into the meeting room to find a beet-red pastor and scowling committee members. Before the DS could even sit down the chairperson launched into his furious tirade.

"He told us he was going to preach from the New Testament! He lied to us and we will not put up with a liar for a pastor!"

The DS looked at the pastor and questioned, "Dwayne, you calmed these people down last week by agreeing to preach from the New Testament for a while, starting with this Sunday. Did you change your mind?"

"Sir," responded Dwayne in a deadpan tone, "I preached from Hebrews chapter 1."

"Exactly!" said an irate member.

Beginning to show a rising anger the DS said, before abruptly adjourning the meeting, "Dear Brothers and Sisters, the Letter to the Hebrews is in the New Testament."

A year later the pastor was forced to move to another church even though his teenagers were in High School. The pastor's family definitely got hurt.

What is striking about the story is that it would have taken only one lay member of the committee to know Hebrews was in the New Testament. Unfortunately, there was not one of the nine members who knew or if they did know they chose not to speak up.

The Importance of Biblical Literacy

People are going to get hurt in church if an entire congregation, especially its leaders, is biblically illiterate. In the U.S. church we have now raised not one, but two generations who cannot put David, Solomon and Saul in the correct chronological order.[28] Worse yet, the majority of laity cannot tell us two modern day applications for our lives from each of these kings. If the biblical stories no longer form the stories and basis for our lives together, is it any wonder that our fellow Christians are hurting one another and tens of millions are fleeing troubled congregations?

There are two primary ways in which much of our teaching and preaching leadership have led us into this time of biblical illiteracy: Modern preaching models and a failure to do discipleship outside the Sunday morning worship service. Each will be examined independently in this chapter and the next, even though they are tightly woven together in a healthy congregation.

Most Sermons No Longer Create Biblical Literacy

Sermons can be divided into four categories in our land. Of course there are preachers who cross over the boundaries between categories, but the strong majority fall soundly into one of the four. It is not the purpose of this chapter to

---

[28] The right order is Saul, David then Solomon. If you had to follow this footnote to find out, please sign up with a serious Bible study group such as Bible Study Fellowship in your area as soon as possible. Obviously your church is not biblically training you.

hold one category up as preaching the Word of God better than the others.

The message of this section is that certain models simply promote biblical literacy among the laity better than other models. With biblical literacy, the people of God tend to leave gossip and manipulation behind and cease to tolerate it. The hurting is diminished. Without biblical literacy, the hurting rate goes up and the people tolerate it so it happens again and again.

The first category is **EXPOSITORY PREACHING**. There's another big word that simply needs explaining. If your preacher stands on the platform or in the pulpit and says, "For the next six months we will be studying the Gospel of Luke. Today we will begin in chapter 1," you are receiving Expository Preaching. When the preacher finishes Luke, the preacher announces the next book of the Bible the congregation will explore together on Sunday mornings. This, in a nutshell, is expositional preaching. For many more details on this model of preaching I suggest John MacArthur's Book, *Rediscovering Expository Preaching*.[29]

Some preachers will take multiple years to get through Luke. Others will take months. A section of the book will be chosen, possibly fifteen verses, and expounded upon (that's where the word expository comes from). If the passage is The Good Samaritan in Luke 10 the preacher will spend the first twenty minutes going verse by verse and educating the congregation on the seven primary messages

---

29 John MacArthur, Richard Mayhue, Robert Thomas and The Master's College Faculty, *Rediscovering Expository Preaching*. Thomas Nelson, 1992.

from this passage for our lives today, from the ridiculousness of legalism to Jesus' stance on racism, to helping those in need. All of those messages are within the story of The Good Samaritan.

The preacher then takes the second twenty minutes or so of the sermon and elaborates on *one* of those messages that Luke originally wanted to express. In a great expository sermon that message is powerfully applied to our lives today.

Discussions in the car going home range from what everyone learned about Luke and the themes of his book to the seven ideas in the passage to the one, primary message the preacher applied to our lives in the end. The people of God are educated, inspired and transformed. Most of these worship services are sixty to ninety minutes long. Strict time limits are only enforced if a second or third worship service is soon to follow in the same worship space. Deep down, those in the car suspect the preacher spent anywhere from fifteen to twenty hours preparing the sermon.

Next comes **BIG IDEA PREACHING**.[30] It is similar to expositional so we can cover it quickly. This preacher is marching through the primary passages of Luke, as well, before moving on to another book of the Bible.

During the week the pastor studies the seven primary messages of the Good Samaritan parable and chooses one of the seven that is the most applicable to the congregation. Let's say it is helping those in need. The pastor

---

[30] Keith Willhite and Scott Gibson, *The Big Idea of Biblical Preaching: Connecting the Bible to People*. Baker Books, 2003.

prepares a sermon strictly on the one big idea for the sermon. Willhite and Gibson's book, *The Big Idea of Biblical Preaching: Connecting the Bible to People,* explains this style well.

The educational, verse by verse section of the expository sermon disappears. Only the one big idea is preached. Discussions in the car driving home are about the one big idea and its application to our modern lives. Those in the car suspect the pastor spent eight to twelve hours preparing the sermon.

The third is **DISTRACTED PREACHING.** This occurs when the congregation does not fulfill its duties as servants to the community and to the hard work of being a congregation. The pastor spends the week dealing with financial reports, problems in the pre-school, attends four meetings, goes to two board meetings in the community or for the denomination, visits in the hospitals every other day and then mows the church lawn on Friday or Saturday. The elders or administrative board have never lovingly told the pastor to spend more time on preparing the sermon and that they would take care of the other issues.

On Thursday, Friday or Saturday the pastor quickly chooses a passage from anywhere in the Bible. The passage is read once and no commentaries or biblical study tools are consulted whatsoever. This method of sermon preparation involves fervent prayer as the pastor begins to beg God for a few stories and illustrations that can be strung together to make up the sermon. The ones that are prepared exclusively on Saturday evenings can be called Saturday Night

Specials because they are mercilessly shot at the congregation the next morning.[31]

These sermons can be long or short as the pastor rambles on in an extemporaneous manner. Driving home in the car people know the pastor only spent two to three hours preparing, and they discuss the need for a new pastor. They seldom, if ever, discuss their own responsibility as laity to take work off the pastor's plate and to hold the pastor accountable for spending more time on sermon preparation.

TOPICAL PREACHING is the most popular form of preaching in our country right now, with distracted preaching coming in a close second. In this model, the pastor contemplates the community and the congregation, prays, and decides on a sermon topic or a series of sermons that falls under the same overarching topic. An eight-week series on forgiveness would be a popular example.

The pastor then opens a Scripture index, looks for that topic, and finds anywhere from one to ten Bible passages that support what the pastor wishes to say. During the sermon the pastor stresses this topic. Some pastors preach from one passage and delve into that passage well, explaining its author and context. Others bounce from one verse to another like a rabbit going through tall grass, never stopping to explain the context of the verse or the original intent, or even the name of the original biblical author. All

---

31   'Saturday Night Special' is slang for a handgun which is inexpensive, poorly made and of a small caliber. They are easily disposed of after a crime is committed. They often do not function well. In 1981 John Hinckley, Jr. used a 22-caliber Saturday Night Special in his failed assassination attempt on Ronald Reagan.

that matters is that the biblical author appears to agree with the message the pastor already decided to preach.

In the car the conversation is about the topic, at best. Often it is about lunch because the pastor already covered everything there is to say about the topic. The pastor's intent was to let people know how to think. It was not to educate or stimulate thought. The congregation suspects the pastor put in anywhere from eight to twenty hours on the sermon and they are happy.

If you are from some traditional churches, you may have noticed that Lectionary Preaching is not listed here as a category. This is the system where the preacher follows a set of biblical passages that repeats every three years. Some preachers use a certain Sunday's biblical passages in an expositional way while others look for one big idea. Other preachers use them but put 2 to 3 hours into their preparation and classify as distracted preachers. I have even heard preachers who read the lectionary texts for that Sunday and then preach a wholly different topical sermon. For those who come from churches that are committed to the lectionary, please choose from one of the four categories in bold which explains how the lectionary texts are used.

Question for Reflection

Draw lines below between each of the most popular sermon styles in the United States today with their ability to help raise up a biblically literate congregation. *Do not rank them based on popularity or which is your favorite.* While drawing lines between the two sides strictly think about which preaching style helps a congregation to become more biblically literate.

Draw lines between the two columns:

Most Effective at Promoting Biblical Literacy	Distracted Preaching
Second Most Effective	Expositional Preaching
Third Most Effective	Topical Preaching
Worst at Promoting Biblical Literacy	Big Idea Preaching

We can all agree that Distracted Preaching is the worst at promoting biblical literacy or any other need a congregation may have. It is sad that it has become so common.

The best at promoting biblical literacy is Expositional Preaching. Sermons are longer but most congregations don't even notice because they leave educated and inspired and thinking about many topics throughout the week.

Big Idea Preaching is still bringing the Scriptures to the people, but the expressed goal of those who promote this style is to inspire and motivate a congregation. Educating a congregation is not the highest value. For this reason, it comes in second in meeting the goal of transforming people from a biblically illiterate generation into biblically literate people.

Topical Preaching is exceedingly popular. Preachers like it because their views get a full airing. People like it because it doesn't require them to mull over the passage during the next week as much. Some of these sermons are tremendously inspiring. However, it clearly comes in third as far as developing biblically literate people.

A Mix

Personally, I believe there are many topics that need to be covered each year within its fifty-two sermons. For this reason, I reserve about twenty percent of sermons, or eleven per year, for topically based sermons. This can be Christmas, Easter, a recent headline in the newspaper or a struggle the community or the congregation is facing, such as the subject of gossip, manipulation and churches hurting people. Guest preachers fit into this twenty percent of sermons, too. There are also times when a preacher needs to share key vision for the future that has been confirmed by the board or elders, and it is now time to bring this vision to the congregation. The key to building a biblically literate congregation is to keep at least the other eighty percent, or about forty-one sermons per year, as expository sermons.

Remember the phrase, "As goes the pulpit, so goes the church?" If the preacher or preachers at the key worship services each weekend are communicating that biblical literacy is important, then the church will consider biblical literacy to be important. If those in the pulpit or on the platform are communicating that it is of secondary importance, or of no importance, they should not be surprised if they preach for five years and their people cannot tell them the difference between the four Gospels and the letters of St. Paul.

People need a biblical education. If the sermon is only about inspiration and application and never about education, then our people will not be educated, and we can only hope that they are inspired.

Learning the material within the Holy Scriptures and learning how to apply it to one's own life, all on one's own without help, is of infinite value. The Scriptures become my story. I can do ethics all by myself, even without my pastor in the room telling me exactly how to think. I become an ethical person with a solid biblical foundation for making ethical choices. My life is transformed and I would never think about hurting someone in the church wantonly and flagrantly.

Most us reading this book have sat in church meetings where ridiculous statements were made like Pastor Dwayne and the DS experienced. Unprepared, undisciplined, biblically illiterate people can turn a group the wrong way. They can bring a lot of hurt to a lot of people and steer a congregation away from God's path.

Many Christians are praying for a revival of Christianity in the U.S. As Steve Lawson has noted in *Famine in the Land*, there has been a lack of preaching which produces spiritual maturity and depth in our land. The result has been a famine of the full Word of God. He writes, "If a reformation is to come to the church, it must be preceded by a reformation of the pulpit."[32]

Philip Jacob Spener writes, "Where the Word of God is neglected, real and true religion collapses." The opposite

---

[32] Steven J. Lawson, *Famine in the Land*, Moody Publishers, Chicago, 2003. Page 17.

PAIN BECAUSE THE SCRIPTURES ARE NOT TAUGHT

is also true: "The more at home the Word of God is among us, the more we shall bring about faith and its fruits."[33]

If you are personally hungry for the preached Word of God and are not receiving it regularly in your life in a way that builds your biblical literacy, please consider the following websites. From them you can listen to hundreds of high quality sermons from preachers who represent the Faithful Church. This list is far from exhaustive and many other resources exist for sermons that can help build your biblical knowledge. During your commute or some other portion of your day you can bring biblical literacy into your life even if your local church is not helping greatly in this area.

- John McArthur. He has been preaching long enough that he has preached through all of the New Testament and a great deal of the Old Testament, piece by piece. https://www.gty.org/resources/sermons

- R.C. Sproul http://www.ligonier.org/learn/sermons/

- Steve Lawson (a semi-expositional preacher) http://www.onepassionministries.org/download-sermons/

Some may ask the question, 'Can't biblical education happen in other forums?' Is it really that important to biblically educate from the pulpit?

---

[33] Philip Jacob Spener, *Pia Desideria*, Translated by Theodore G. Tappert, Fortress Press, 1964, Originally published in 1675, pages 79 & 87.

There is no other place in the life of the church that allows a message to reach such a large portion of the congregation. Even if small groups and Sunday School classes are teaching the Bible, there is no reason to believe the rest of the congregation will become, over time, biblically literate. Also, with biblical literacy as one of the goals of preaching, the process simply happens faster and in a deeper way.

Intermission II

Yesterday was an incredible day. While on a short vacation to see my parents I visited a Faithful Church. I had the honor of serving this church a few years back and it has grown by 300 per weekend since then!

Seeing old friends was sweet. The music had deep, meaningful lyrics and reached my heart and my mind. From experience I know their choice of music at all four services are exactly what the demographic around them is wanting. The music is directed at the community and not the desires of long-standing members. Meanwhile, the lyrics were centered on Christ and our service to the Lord. The sermon was straight from the Scriptures and brought us to understand the original intent of the biblical authors and the application for today. The announcements and worship bulletin had a tremendous amount of mission opportunities and discipleship/growth opportunities.

In the sanctuary were people in wheelchairs, a homeless person and teenagers who I know from experience had been on drugs while in junior high school. These three groups got more hugs than anyone else. I heard a first-time visitor say, "This place is amazing and a little bit scary!" I agreed with her.

Later in the day the former pastor and I spoke on the phone. He was reviewing the first seven chapters of this book and he was very straightforward. There were four areas where my own blindness kept me from seeing those issues well. He was loving and blunt, as he always is. This book is better because of that phone call. I am a better person because of that phone call.

The Faithful Church is so beautiful.

Moving Forward

We have seen why people are getting hurt in local churches today. We have seen the need to develop disciples and become a more biblically literate people. As we do so, American Civil Religion will hurt fewer people because more congregations will move to be part of the Faithful Church. Now we'll look deeper at how to do this, practically speaking.

CHAPTER 12

Discipleship and Biblical Literacy

Leviticus 19:1, 2
The Lord said to Moses,
"Speak to the entire assembly
of Israel and say to them:
'Be holy because I,
the Lord your God, am holy.'"

The two beautiful verses above come immediately after the Lord says to Moses in chapter 18 that God does not want the people to do the detestable things the people in the Middle East were doing at that time. The message given by God goes against the grain of the surrounding culture. Be holy as God is holy. No matter the age, this statement will be countercultural.

When we welcome one person into the life of the Body of Christ we cannot forget that they bring the detestable parts of the culture with them. Bring a hundred new people into the Body and suddenly we are looking at a massive threat to any congregation, unless there is an intentional process of discipleship. If just five percent of the hundred are gossips, manipulators or power brokers, our congregation is doomed.

In addition to being detestable, our culture is deeply hypocritical. Most gossips and manipulators thrive out there in the culture. When the church, out of a sense of openness and hospitality invites them in, these same gossips and manipulators give the church a bad name! What the culture tolerates out there, the culture condemns when it occurs in the church. The church is held to a higher standard.

The good news is that it should be. Everyone has a right to expect more from the Body of Christ. They have a right to expect it to be a light unto the world! Without a careful membership process and an intentional discipleship process we will never be the light the world expects us to be and a place of holy behavior *as the Lord* expects us to be.

The Billy Graham Evangelistic Association has a key rule. They will not come into a town or city and do a crusade unless there are enough local congregations willing to step up and do the hard discipling of new believers after the crusade ends. Anywhere from dozens to hundreds of congregations are trained to do discipleship.

Those who come to the front during the crusade to accept Christ are given reading material and a card to fill out. Once filled out these cards are given to local congregations as a sacred trust to follow up and to disciple.

Yet intentional discipleship programs are few and far between. I live in a small city in the Bible Belt of the Mid-West with fifty thousand residents. I have taken a look at

DISCIPLESHIP AND BIBLICAL LITERACY

every church with more than 125 in worship on Sunday. Not a single one has an intentional, planned, printed discipleship program for new believers. My prayer is that your congregation is an exception. Most are not.

Discipleship and biblical literacy begin with the pulpit or platform and flows to the congregation. It is a value that is transferred. If the key teaching leadership in the church does not have a passion for it from the pulpit, it will likely not happen during the week.

The few congregations that try to do discipleship often make the mistake of purchasing pre-packaged discipleship material. At best there is proof that the material has worked in one place and time, the author's. There is no guarantee it will work in the radically different cultural context of the church that bought the packaged program 1,500 miles away. After trying a few pre-packaged discipleship programs the congregation gives up.

Some pastors have not learned how to form a discipleship program for their *particular* congregation. This chapter will explain the simple basics for doing so. It is not a package for your church to buy. It is a **process** for your church to form a discipleship program that fits *your community*, *your church* and *your resources*.

Step 1: Define the Disciple Your Congregation Wants to Raise up.

The word disciple is tossed around a great deal in congregations in the United States. To make sure we are all on the same page, let's define what makes up a discipled follower of Christ. Then we can determine how to help people get to this point. Here are some thoughts to help with your own Step 1 that you can do on a separate sheet. While your definition of a disciple may be different than mine, here are some thoughts:

The goal:

- With the help of a Christian leader or a small group, the discipleship candidate has examined their inner, private life for addictions and destructive habits. They have opened their lives to a Christian leader or small group and asked them to address lovingly and directly any negative areas that they cannot see.

DISCIPLESHIP AND BIBLICAL LITERACY

- The person has been introduced to different areas of the Holy Scriptures, such as the Gospels, the Letters of Paul, Genesis/Exodus, the Historical Books, and the Prophetic Writings. The person understands how to read each of these areas of Scripture as the original author meant for them to be read.

- Basic concepts of how to read the Bible, such as one passage helping us to understand another passage, are understood so that frequent Bible reading by the disciple is enjoyable and understandable.

- The person is actively reading the Scriptures, with a plan, in a regular and frequent manner.

- Broken relationships, such as divorce or estrangement from family, have been examined and healing is occurring. New conflict management skills, which do not involve gossip and manipulation, are developed. The new disciple has accepted a congregational covenant of behavior.

- The person knows how to pray and is comfortable doing it.

- The person has discovered their giftedness for ministry, the ways God works through them, and is actively in service to the congregation and/or the community.

- The person has been baptized and made a public proclamation of their faith.

- The person understands the importance of Christian fellowship and is in regular and frequent connection with the Body of Christ. The lone wolf spiritual growth mentality is gone.

- Following the teachings of Jesus, the person has committed their heart, their mind, their calendar and their finances to the Kingdom.

- The person has accepted their role as a light to the world and is a personal supporter of justice on various levels in their personal and societal life.

- The person understands how to do natural, personal evangelism.

- After having been discipled, the person understands their role in discipling and mentoring others in the future.

- Additionally, there are expectations that each pastor of a congregation has for their flock. These have been communicated and the person is respecting them or graciously agreeing to be part of another congregation.

Questions for Reflection

Do you agree with this list?
What would you add or subtract?

_____
_____
_____
_____
_____
_____
_____
_____

What would you re-phrase?

_____
_____
_____
_____
_____
_____
_____
_____

Now write your own list for Step 1 on a separate sheet of paper. This is the first and most important step for designing a discipleship program. We have to know where we are going before we can write a plan to get there.

Step 2: What type of people will enter this Discipleship Program?

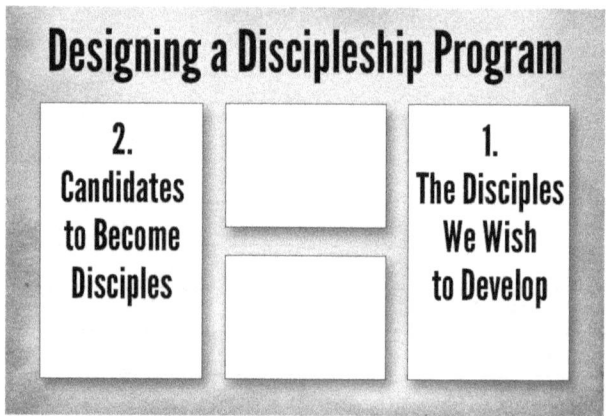

Each congregation lives in a different cultural context. In Step 2 we admit this reality and it allows us to have a developed plan (coming up in Step 4) that takes into account educational and socio-economic differences, and a host of other issues that will affect the discipleship plan. If our people are humble readers, then assigning them Bonhoeffer's *Cost of Discipleship* will have them dropping out quickly. In a highly-educated region we will need some challenging material to keep people's interest.

For instance, in a discipleship design project I am currently working on for a pastoral friend, the candidates to become discipled are:

- Rural

- 23% have no High School Diploma

- 13.7% have a Bachelor's Degree

- 91% Literacy Rate

- The median income is $32,002 per household[34]

The information above was found in a simple Internet search with the name of the town, the state and the word, "demographics." If the pastor and I attempt to design a discipleship program for this church without taking these facts into account, the plan will fail. Opening a packaged discipleship program from a church in New York City will fail, too. Step 2 is crucial because it connects the plan to be made with the actual people to be discipled.

On a separate sheet of paper, write down everything you can think of about your community for Step 2. Let the demographic studies which are free on the internet help your thinking. Write down anything about your congregation and your community that would in any way shape the nature and details of your discipleship program.

Don't write that discipleship plan, yet! We still have one more step.

---

34 City-Data.com information for Plymouth, Indiana at http://www.city-data.com/city/Plymouth-Indiana.html July 28, 2015.

Step 3: List Your Resources

It takes people resources to do a discipleship program. Paying and housing seminary professors for your discipleship program is probably not within your means. You *do* have lots of resources even if you don't think you do. Consider the following possibilities:

- The Pastor and the Pulpit. Once the plan is written in Step 4, the pastor may choose to prepare a sermon on one of the topics from time to time. Ask any high school student to video record it and put it on YouTube.com. With the URL (the internet address) for the video the link can be sent to disciple candidates to watch along with three questions for them to answer by e-mail. YouTube can be about more than cute cats playing the piano. It can contain pieces of your discipleship program.

    It is so easy that high school teachers regularly make assignments for students that involve preparing videos on YouTube.com. The disciple

DISCIPLESHIP AND BIBLICAL LITERACY

candidate watches the video, answers the questions and then someone in the discipleship program reads those answers and e-mails the learner. Credit is given for work the disciple candidate did on their smartphone during their lunch hour. Please stop dragging people into the church building for the learning of simple facts. Modern people don't like it.

- Is the pastor willing to teach some classes or mentor a few people?

- Associate Pastors or Retired Pastors. Are they willing to be involved with the discipleship program?

- Those with the spiritual gift of teaching in the congregation who are theologically trusted are a resource.

- Is there a budget that may be used to purchase components of discipleship (such as the Alpha program), understanding that no purchased program can fulfill all the needs of a particular congregation's discipleship needs. *Some* elements from other congregations and published material can be used as components.

- Are there laity with the spiritual gift of being a pastor (natural shepherding gifts) who can meet one-on-one with people to discuss their habits and addictions? The word "pastor" has come to mean the leader of a congregation. When St. Paul used the word he meant a person who is naturally gifted by the Holy Spirit to mentor and shepherd others. Every congregation has many, many of these people. How many would be willing to mentor new disciples?

- Is there anyone in the congregation who has overcome drugs, alcohol, or porn addictions or who can help with financial or marital counseling?

- Are there existing healthy small groups where someone can grow? Are there leaders for new small groups?

- Are there nearby congregations that have resources your congregation does not that would be willing to help?

- The existing church building schedule may have natural slots for group meetings. Possibly Sunday morning when the kids are already in the kid's program or on Wednesday evenings. Adult discipleship candidates need time away from their kids. Are there educational rooms and times available?

- Are there volunteers in the children's program who could minister to kids for an hour or two while the parents are in a discipleship class or small group?

- What percentage of the discipleship candidates have access to the internet at home, work or through their smartphone? Yes, there is terrible stuff on the web. There are also classes on How to Read the Bible or Basic Christian Beliefs. Many are completely free. When you find a great one, can your people access it?

Write any and all resources you can think of that can possibly be used to help disciple new Christians – and those who always thought they were Christians – but who never received discipleship training. Write each one down on a sheet of paper for Step 3: Resources.

Step 4: The Plan

Designing a Discipleship Program

2. Candidates to Become Disciples	3. Resources	1. The Disciples We Wish to Develop
	4. The Plan	

Please notice where the writing of the plan, Step 4, sits in the diagram. It is between Steps 1, 2 and 3. It is only when the first three steps are done, and done thoroughly, that we start writing the actual discipleship plan. By doing the steps in order, the plan will make sense for the context in which you minister, the resources you have, and most importantly, the goal (Step 1) that you want your disciple candidates to reach.

A solid plan has different components. Please don't fall into the common trap of making everything a class. There are four components to a healthy discipleship plan for a congregation.

- Prayer. For the person and with the person. Prayer retreats are a great idea, too. We teach prayer by example, doing it *with* people, not having a class.

- Classes. Traditionally this has been labor and time intensive. With people's busy schedules, a discipleship program can hit the rocks and break apart if someone has to come to the church building at 7p.m. and stay until 9p.m. every Tuesday.

    Classes that appear on smartphones, tablets and computer screens during one's lunch hour are far more accessible. If a certain piece of material, such as a three-hour course on the spiritual disciplines, needs to be together in a classroom, make it so. If it is simply a 90-minute class on the letters of St. Paul, let Dr. Expert in the Subject teach it to your people for free by the Internet. Spend an hour searching for a great video and use it a hundred or a thousand times.

    Online education, done well, is not the wave of the future. It is already very much here. You can find a high-quality video segment much faster than you can form your own lesson plan and teach it.

- Use conferences that come through your area or denominational opportunities. If a discipleship candidate discovers their spiritual gifts and wants to work with teenagers, get them connected with a Youth Specialties or Group conference coming to the area. Let them experience the power of amazing parachurch training opportunities.

- Mentoring. This can be done one-on-one or in small group settings.

    It is the lack of this component that hurts a large part of discipleship programs. If a candidate never deals with their addictions and bad habits they will never be a true disciple or truly be free in Christ. If they have a habit of gossiping and manipulating, possibly because of a mental health issue, you may never know about it and help them to overcome it if there is not a mentoring component. You may even unwittingly bring them into congregational leadership and damage the church profoundly.

    Here are some suggested questions for mentoring:

    - As you look at the holiness of God, what are the most obvious ways that you fall short of God's holiness?

- Do you have broken relationships in your past?

It can be tempting to have each discipleship candidate meet with a pastor in the church to discuss these issues. Ultimately, this approach is unsustainable and keeps the laity from being the laity. Our society is still at the stage where it is best that women are mentored by women and men are mentored by men.

When your first graduates come out of the program, make sure the church celebrates their completion of the program. This can be a great day in the life of the congregation!

The world outside our congregations is full of gossips. It is full of manipulators. It is full of people with low- and medium-grade mental disorders. The world *will* come into the Church. A well-thought-through discipleship program is a key safety net for your congregation, as well as a biblical mandate (Matthew 28:16-20). Your people will be transformed by the program and leave their church-destructive behavior behind. Without a discipleship program tailored to the reality of your community, people will get hurt on a very regular basis.

CHAPTER 13

A Gift: Standards for Christian Leadership

> *1 Timothy 3:14-15*
> *Although I hope to come to you soon, I am writing you these instructions so that, if I am delayed, you will know how people ought to conduct themselves in God's household, which is the church of the living God, the pillar and foundation of the truth.*

Moral standards for church leadership, lay and clergy, have slipped in the United States over the last seventy years. This has not occurred in a vacuum. As American society has experienced the sexual revolution and the dropping of moral expectations for all citizens, the church has suffered the same fate. In other words, we followed the world.

Of all the institutions in our society, it seems that only the military has maintained, generally speaking, relatively high moral expectations in certain areas. A soldier or officer is promptly booted out after the first Driving Under the Influence conviction or failed drug test for marijuana under the Zero Tolerance Policy. There is bad behavior and then there is a consequence.

The church is not in need of a biblically graceless approach to fallen leaders. Both the DUI soldier and the pedophile priest need the church as a place of healing. The question is whether or not bad behavior, which hurts people and drives them away from congregations in droves, has consequences. Are we willing to choose and train church leaders carefully and set them aside for a time of healing, or do we just shrug at clear immorality in leadership?

Our society expects more from the church in the area of leadership standards, and we should expect more of ourselves. There are structural and theological reasons why many churches have slipped into American Civil Religion.

The bylaws of some mainline denominations call for a minimum number of lay leaders in a local congregation. When a congregation has seventy-five in worship each weekend, and thirty mandatory lay leadership slots to fill, a grave problem is the result. The nominating committee will begin to ask unqualified, spiritually immature people to become leaders. That quota of leaders must be met. Meanwhile, the Pastoral Epistles call us to a quality of leadership over quantity.

Finding youth counselors can be a challenge. Every pastor knows that without a children's program and a youth program, attracting new families to the church is nearly impossible. When people volunteer, there is a

A GIFT: STANDARDS FOR CHRISTIAN LEADERSHIP

great temptation to say "yes." Asking questions about their moral life might cost us a youth counselor. This is especially true of churches that are not intentionally discipling new members and helping them to find their area of Kingdom service.

Then there is the definition of grace. Grace in many churches means being nice, soft and sweet. In the Bible it means something radically different. It is every action of God to bring God's people from sin and separation back into relationship with God. Everything God does is grace.

This includes the story of Ananias and Sapphira in Acts chapter 5. God killed the two of them, in part, to remind the early church that it was still under discipline for immoral behavior. It is supreme arrogance on our part to re-define grace to make it what we want it to be, all sugary and nice, and ignore the clear definition of grace in the Word of God. God is forgiving and patient, but God is God and we are not. God is ultimately our judge, here and after this life.

It is not grace to neglect asking the potential youth counselor if she or he is sexually active outside of the biblical definition of marriage. Once we find out a youth counselor has moved in with their fiancé, it is not grace to "let it slide" for three months until they are married. I have been advised to do this and been told I was lacking in grace when I refused.

Philip Jacob Spener lived in a different time, but it had a lot of similarities to ours. In 1675 he wrote, "You know when you see a tree whose leaves are faded and withering that there is something wrong with the roots; so when you see that people are undisciplined, you must realize that no doubt their priests are not holy."[35]

From Ohio comes the statement of a layperson: "Our stewardship chairperson has been married three times inside this very church. His current mistress used to be his second wife. Everyone knows he is doing it, and giving is way down this year."

If blank lines were provided for you to write stories you know concerning church leaders who escaped appropriate personal growth opportunities, also known as church discipline, there would be a need for many, many lines for most of you.

Somewhere along the way we allowed church leaders to escape loving discipline. The ability to discipline leaders became almost nonexistent for all but the gravest of offenses, and sometimes not even then. When we choose new leaders, we don't want to ask the hard questions about their personal morality.

The Pastoral Epistles

The Church, the Bride of Christ, has been given a great gift from God. It sits within every church and almost every home. Regrettably, it is an unopened present with dust on it in churches that are flat or declining in attendance. It is the gift of the Pastoral Epistles, I and II Timothy and Titus in the New Testament.

---

[35] Philip Jacob Spener, *Pia Desideria*, Translated by Theodore G. Tappert, Fortress Press, 1964, page 44.

A GIFT: STANDARDS FOR CHRISTIAN LEADERSHIP

When was the last time you heard a sermon from these letters from Paul? There are too many members in our churches who couldn't tell you whether they are in the Old or New Testament! Yet the blessing they represent from God on moral standards for church leaders cannot be overstated. If we open the present, study these small letters and apply them to our local churches, the number of people hurt would be far fewer.

The occasion for these short letters from Paul was his desire to take years of pastoral experience and pour it into the younger pastors, Timothy and Titus. These letters were so filled with the Holy Spirit that the early church fell in love with them and included them in the canon of the New Testament. There the gift sits, waiting to be unwrapped by modern-day churches.

Paul writes not of high educational standards for leaders that some denominations and movements have adopted over the last seventy years. Paul doesn't write about how church leaders should develop their skills and how many church growth books they should read.

He writes instead of the value of Holiness when we choose our pastors, our staff, our leaders of the laity and our small group leaders. We are to be holy as God is holy. We are to be cleansed by the Holy Spirit in our motivations and desires in life. We don't become perfect, but we do become changed, and the change is clear to those inside and outside the church. Until this happens, Paul does not want a person to be chosen for leadership.

I do not expect you to agree with each interpretation offered here. If you simply engage in significant personal thought about how to apply these passages to the modern church, I will be a very happy author. We will look at I Timothy 3:1-7, but I recommend all of these three letters be read by each of us and reapplied to our leadership recruitment and training at least once a year.

Paul is writing I Timothy to the younger leader, Timothy.[36] It was written toward the end of Paul's life between 64 and 68 AD, during the reign of Nero. [37]

In the NIV translation, the passage is one paragraph. These seven verses are divided here into the segments to be discussed regarding qualifications for church leaders.

1 Timothy 3:1-7

Here is a trustworthy saying: Whoever aspires to be an overseer desires a noble task.

Now the overseer is to be above reproach,

faithful to his wife,

temperate,

self-controlled,

respectable,

---

[36] There are theories of non-Pauline authorship of I Timothy. They are unconvincing. Church history has always ascribed these three letters as being from Paul as he shared wisdom with younger pastors.
[37] W.A. Elwell, *Evangelical Commentary on the Bible* (Vol. 3, 1 Ti 1:1). Grand Rapids, MI: Baker Book House. (1995).

A GIFT: STANDARDS FOR CHRISTIAN LEADERSHIP

hospitable,

able to teach,

not given to drunkenness,

not violent but gentle, not quarrelsome,

not a lover of money.

He must manage his own family well and see that his children obey him, and he must do so in a manner worthy of full respect. (If anyone does not know how to manage his own family, how can he take care of God's church?)

He must not be a recent convert, or he may become conceited and fall under the same judgment as the devil.

He must also have a good reputation with outsiders, so that he will not fall into disgrace and into the devil's trap.

We begin with a general interpretation regarding the entire passage. Is Paul giving us a checklist? If the potential small group leader's 3-year old disobeys in public should we pass over them for leadership? Certainly not! We have a first century list of moral values that we are certainly able to add on to. If a potential youth counselor has had multiple abortions or driven a woman to an abortion clinic, and remains unrepentant, this would be a problem for most churches. It is not in Paul's first century list but it certainly can be in ours. *What we read is the overall sense that holiness and humility are important in choosing leadership.*

Now the overseer is to be above reproach

We begin with the word "overseer" in verse 1. To whom does this passage apply? Regrettably some translations have gone directly from the Greek word *episkopos* to the English word *bishop*, implying in modern English an overseer of dozens or hundreds of congregations. The context is the key. These churches planted by Paul were small relative to today and one per city or town. Paul was the overseer of all the churches he planted. If we want to use the modern word "bishop," then Paul would have been the bishop. Timothy was the pastor of the church and the list is not about him, so it must mean another tier of leadership. The best definition of "overseer" would be a small group leader, youth leader or associate pastor. Church staff would be overseers.

The phrase, "above reproach" is explained well by Walter Lock: "Not liable to criticism as he would be if he failed in any of these qualities."[38] F.F. Bruce terms it as "free from those sins that mark the society and the age in which he lives."[39]

---

38 Walter Lock, *The Pastoral Epistles (1 and 2 Timothy and Titus)*. Edinburgh: T & T Clark, 1924. Page 36.
39 F.F. Bruce, *The International Bible Commentary*. Grand Rapids, MI: Marshall/Pickering/Zondervan, 1986), Page 1478.

A GIFT: STANDARDS FOR CHRISTIAN LEADERSHIP

In choosing leaders, our motto has become: "Don't ask, don't tell." This is vastly different than asking enough questions to make sure a potential leader is "above reproach."

Faithful to his wife

Paul was probably not married, so interpreting this phrase as a prohibition against single leaders is highly unlikely. The church needs to embrace chaste, single leaders as it embraces faithful, married leaders.

Different movements address the issue of divorced leaders differently, but it is important to realize the Scriptures do allow for divorce and re-marriage in limited circumstances, such as adultery. Other movements respect addiction or abuse as legitimate causes that allow for re-marriage.

The Pastoral Epistles and the rest of Scripture are interpreted in different ways on marriage, divorce and re-marriage. It is good to discuss these issues internally and respect the position of the church.

What is dangerous for the Church is to ask these hard questions of those seeking ordination but to neglect them when choosing lay leadership or staff. Once again, many are using Don't Ask, Don't Tell as a way to avoid awkward conversations. With this approach it is not surprising when our church leadership is the same as the world outside the church, and the values of the world quickly come into the church.

We need to be asking if the potential leader for a Bible study is different than our society in general in the area of sexual purity and considering marriage to be sacred. In singleness, are they chaste? In marriage, are they attentive and caring toward their spouse? If you asked to see the potential leader's web browsing history would they allow it?

Temperate, self-controlled, respectable, hospitable

Notice that these are not educational standards. One does not have to be a business owner or an officer in the military. These are moral characteristics.

Able to teach

The fifth quality, "able to teach," involves skills and calling. An overseer must certainly have the propensity to pass on advice and doctrine to enquirers. "The church has been at its weakest when this basic requirement has been absent in its leaders," says Guthrie, a commentator who has studied this passage.[40]

The difference between the list of characteristics for overseers and the list for deacons is different in this one key area. The Word of God is what we do in the church. We share it, we teach it and we mentor with it in mind. We are not exactly an educational institution, but we are not far off from it, either.

Principals of schools are former teachers. Presidents of colleges are professors. It is no surprise that St. Paul is reminding us that the key leaders of Faithful Churches are "apt to teach." If a person is not, they are simply destined to serve honorably in other areas of the life of the church. Leaders at key lay positions need to be capable teachers.

---

[40] D. Guthrie, *Pastoral Epistles: An Introduction and Commentary* (Vol. 14, p. 96). Downers Grove, IL: InterVarsity Press, (1990).

A GIFT: STANDARDS FOR CHRISTIAN LEADERSHIP

Not given to drunkenness

Drunkenness, addiction or abuse is clearly not appropriate for potential church leaders. Denominations, movements and local churches need to clearly communicate their stance on drinking alcohol.

What is less clear is private drinking. In too many movements stemming from John Wesley or from the Baptists, the official manual says one thing, but the hush-hush advice from many leaders is to privately indulge. For potential young leaders this creates confusion and should be avoided. It also teaches disrespect for the official covenants and documents under which we agree to serve. If your church says you may drink, then drink in moderation. If your church says you may not drink, then don't drink.

Not violent but gentle, not quarrelsome

Have you met people who love drama? Give them a potentially tense situation and the vast majority of the time they will help it explode. Police officers and school teachers are taught to de-escalate verbal situations. Officers who cannot do so are increasingly referred to as bad cops by society. The ability to de-escalate a situation naturally is the approach we look for in church leadership.

Working with upset people is clearly a part of leadership. Our members and attendees are under tremendous stress, have made poor life choices, are on lots of prescription drugs – then they come to church. They criticize the color of the new carpet in the sanctuary with an over-the-top tone of voice. How the biblical church leader receives their rant determines whether or not people get hurt in the church. Drama kings and drama queens need not apply. The ability to de-escalate a verbal situation is becoming more and more important in church leadership.

John McArthur states in his commentary on this passage:

> Considerate, genial, gracious, quick to pardon failure, and one who does not hold a grudge. **Peaceable.** "Peaceful," "reluctant to fight"; one who does not promote disunity or disharmony.[41]

Regrettably, I have met many church staff persons who openly and publically disagreed with the lead pastor, in public, on issues of vision and the implementation of that vision. Some devolved into public criticisms of the pastor on a personal level. Church leaders need to value unity and express their disagreements with one another *in private*.

Not a lover of money

Our society loves money. Personal value is often determined by how much money one makes. Is it any surprise that these values have crept insidiously into church leadership?

On the other hand, church leadership that does not care for and honor the pastor with at least a cost-of-living raise each year, and preferably more, is asking for trouble. Three years without a raise and the pastor or staff person is likely to be tempted by the enemy to feel less self-assured

---

[41] John MacArthur, Jr. (2006). *The MacArthur study Bible: New American Standard Bible.* (1 Ti 3:3). Nashville, TN: Thomas Nelson Publishers.

and less loved by the congregation. Church staff have human emotions, too.

For unpaid church leaders, please know that chasing after money and neglecting your Kingdom of God responsibilities is not why you were chosen by God for leadership. Family and work are important in our lives. There are entirely too many local church lay leaders who give frightfully few hours to the work of the Lord. If you are a leader in the Kingdom then lead.

He must manage his own family well and see that his children obey him, and he must do so in a manner worthy of full respect. (If anyone does not know how to manage his own family, how can he take care of God's church?) He must not be a recent convert, or he may become conceited and fall under the same judgment as the devil.

"He must not be a recent convert" is not defined as far as a number of months or years. Some come into the faith hungry to learn and grow and are ready for leadership in a year. These are the few and far between. Most take longer. A good modern way of expressing this prerequisite to Christian leadership would be the phrase spiritual maturity.

A clear connection exists here with the overall theme in the Pastoral Epistles of avoiding false teaching. If it is to be avoided, then recent converts should not be placed in roles that include teaching authority, such as an overseer. It is too easy for them to fall into one of the heresies of this culture if they are not yet grounded in the apostolic teachings.[42]

There is also the issue of conceit as a part of the "or he may become" clause. The author of 1 Timothy is clearly connecting the first part of the sentence – about leaders not being recent converts – with the second about conceit. When a person arrives at a position of authority before they have enough spiritual maturity, we are doing neither them nor the church a favor by placing them in a position where conceit can flourish.[43]

The use of "the Devil" makes it clear that St. Paul believes this to be the work of the Devil. If the leader is spiritually mature, there are more defenses built up against the enemy's attacks.

He must also have a good reputation with outsiders, so that he will not fall into disgrace and into the devil's trap.

When a person has fallen, it does not help them to keep the pressures of leadership on their shoulders. What is also at issue here is what is best for the entire church. The Bride of Christ must be high in our considerations when we deal with moral failings. Grace and mercy upon the person are not the only issues to be considered. Serious consideration must be given to the grace that God wishes to bestow upon the congregation so that it continues to be a healthy, well-balanced congregation that can grow in depth and in number. Considering only the comfort of

---

42 William F. Taylor, "1 Timothy 3:1-7: The Public Side of Ministry." Trinity Seminary Review 4, No. 1 (Spring 1992) Page 9.
43 Walter Lock, Page 39.

the fallen leader and his or her family and not considering the needs of the congregation would be incomprehensible to St. Paul.

These seven verses are a great gift, as are all 13 chapters of the Pastoral Epistles, I and II Timothy and Titus. They are worthy of reading, study and debate. If we are planning to train potential or existing leaders in the church, I heartily recommend these letters as we form the core of the training.

As we return to biblical standards for leadership, the number of people getting hurt in local churches will drop dramatically.

CHAPTER 14

Transforming the Church's Staff

1 Peter 5:2-3
Be shepherds of God's flock that is under your care, watching over them – not because you must, but because you are willing, as God wants you to be, not pursuing dishonest gain, but eager to serve; not lording it over those entrusted to you, but being examples to the flock.

Julie had been the paid, part-time youth director for seven years. Two Sundays of every month, the youth group came together for ninety minutes to play board games. There were no lessons, and Bibles were not present. Then they went home. Once a year, the youth line item of the church budget provided for the group to visit Disney World for the weekend. Worst of all, Julie had not been to a worship service, at that church or any other, in five years. She liked to sleep in on Sunday mornings.

When the new pastor arrived it turned out he had two junior high kids. After a month he began to ask awkward questions about the youth group and discovered its weak nature. Julie used the excuse of having a full-time job as the reason she could not meet with the pastor to discuss the issues – ever. Remember, Julie was a part-time paid staff person who refused to meet with the pastor.

The pastor was quickly informed that Julie, through blood or marriage, was related to all three influential families in the church. She needed that part-time income to make ends meet. She would not be able to pay her bills without it. She obviously felt no accountability to the pastor.

In the same church, Brenda was the choir director. She had been in that position twenty-six years. When the area around the church transitioned to a younger demographic with lots of apartments, Brenda did not transition the church's style of music. Thursday evenings were not only for choir practice, but also Brenda's soapbox to proclaim what was wrong with the church, the pastor and to explain how everything should be. Again, there was no accountability.

Without the resignations of Julie and Brenda the church had little hope of attracting the younger families and singles within the area. With their resignations encouraged, the blame was placed on the pastor and it was only a matter of time before he was asked to leave. At least the next pastor would have a chance to reach the community from a stronger position.

At a different church, it was war between the new pastor and most of the dozen existing staff members. He and they were headed completely different directions, and most of the staff opposed his principal initiative, a new church start. Political camps formed. The church went from 750 per weekend to 350 per weekend in four years. Every church within ten miles was receiving their wounded members. It was a battle for power within the staff, and the Body of Christ lost.

Power struggles within the staff of a congregation can be devastating. In some churches, the lead pastor is not the most influential person in the congregation. Sometimes it is a staff member who knows how to use gossip and manipulation to gain and hold on to power.

Because church staff, especially lead pastors, represent the church in a recognizable and obvious way, their ability to hurt people is magnified by ten. If José is the pastor, people don't say, "José hurt me," they say, "The church hurt me." The higher one goes in church leadership the more our comments, mistakes and sins have the potential to hurt others.

Paid church staff represents the church in a way no one else can. This is one of the reasons 1 Timothy 3:2 says, "Now the overseer is to be above reproach..." as the first of all the moral requirements of a church leader. Staff are to be beyond reproach.

In the lines below write your own story about power battles within a church staff or a lack of healthy accountability. Don't forget to write about the damage to the congregation.

_____
_____
_____
_____

CHURCHES THAT HURT

_____
_____
_____
_____
_____
_____
_____
_____
_____
_____
_____
_____
_____
_____

It has been said that all sin falls under four categories: Sex, money, power and glory. While church leadership is occasionally tempted by sex, money or glory, the vast majority of the struggles within church staffs involve power. It is also where lay and clergy get hurt with tremendous frequency and everyone around them becomes collateral damage.

Dietrich Bonhoeffer, the German Christian martyr who stood against Hitler, writes in *Life Together* about Jesus and the Twelve Disciples:

"There arose a reasoning among them, which of them should be the greatest" (Luke 9:46). We know who it is that sows this thought in the Christian community[44]... Thus at the very beginning of Christian fellowship there is engendered an invisible, often unconscious, life-and-death contest. "There arose a reasoning among them": this is enough to destroy a fellowship.

Hence it is vitally necessary that every Christian community from the very outset face this dangerous enemy squarely, and eradicates it. There is no time to lose here.[45]

No congregation can flourish if the staff is involved in a power struggle. It has to be eradicated or the people of God, and the staff, will pay a terrible price.

Solutions

Here are a few solutions to staff conflicts stemming from power struggles:

- Begin with prayer. Any congregation that does not pray for unity and peace among its staff is asking for the enemy to come in and start trouble. Staff are open to human temptation and need to be

---

[44] From the wider context around this passage, Bonhoeffer is referring to Satan.
[45] Bonhoeffer, Dietrich, *Life Together*. Harper One, 1954, Page 90.

protected by prayer. The family that prays together, stays together. The staff that prays together, real, extended prayer, chooses not to fight each other. Staff prayer needs to be measured not in minutes per month but in hours.

- Rev. David McEntire of Lakeland, Florida, suggests a written staff covenant that the staff brainstorms and refines together. The lead pastor asks, "What are the boundaries for our ministry together? What will we do and not do in relationship to each other?" The brainstorming begins and the white board fills up. 'We will not gossip about each other.' 'We will seek the good of the Kingdom before our own good.' Step 2 is to remove a number of the brainstormed items if there is not agreement from the strong majority of the group.

    A week later it is discussed again and finally put on paper. There is Holy Communion and a signing ceremony. It becomes an agreement between the staff on things they will and will not do to one another. If anyone breaks this staff-written covenant the pastor or elders or board may bring about discipline or release them from service based upon their choice to break the staff covenant. After one or two are released from service, the staff takes the yearly writing of the covenant very seriously, as well as holding to its content.

    Rev. McEntire turned around a declining 2,200 person per weekend church with this staff covenant.

After just four months, two staff members had been removed for violating the covenant they had helped to write. The staff began to care for each other and pull the same direction. The church then grew.

- As a congregation interviews a lead pastor or potential new staff member, it should look for evidence that power has been held with an open palm in the past. God gives authority and God takes it away. Glory be to God. If power has been held with a closed fist (grab power and hold it at all cost) in the past, it will probably be held that way in the future unless a clear transformation has occurred. We all have a little Napoleon within us. Middle- and large-sized Napoleons should be avoided.

- Many independent congregations require the staff to sign letters of resignation when a new pastor arrives. At any point in the first six months the new pastor may pull out a letter of resignation and accept it, without question from the board or elders. Only if all of the staff and the lead pastor are headed the same direction can a congregation flourish. There is no question that this is not fair to staff and for this reason extensive severance packages should be provided to allow them to become re-employed in these situations. The good news is that it radically helps with staff unity.

If it comes down to a choice between fairness or a church staff all moving the same direction and flourishing, then the decision is easy to make. Staff serve the Body of Christ, not the other way around. It also avoids ongoing power struggles that hurt too many people in the congregation.

- Staff or pastors who repeatedly use gossip and relational power should be dismissed from the staff and removed from the congregation. Their healing regarding the sin of gossip can take place while they attend a different congregation's worship service. Removing them from just the staff and leaving them in the congregation is the very definition of danger. They can do great harm against the leadership after they are removed from the staff if they stay. The lead pastor may as well take up sky diving without a parachute if the former, gossiping staff member stays in the congregation.

- Elder groups and administrative board members should be actively looking for gossips and manipulators on the church staff at any level, including the lead pastor. These dangerous influences within the core of the congregation should be 'eradicated', as Bonhoeffer writes.

- Church bylaws should clearly explain the board or elder group's authority, as well as that of the lead pastor and any other holder of spiritual authority in the congregation. Unwritten authority can cause tremendous problems in the future.

- Bylaws cannot be an inch and a half thick or only church lawyers will know what is in them, and they will argue about how to interpret them. The congregation or denomination will form into political parties with each side thumping their copy of the bylaws. This is where most mainline denominations are today. Keep it simple but complete.

- Bylaws should not be in a filing cabinet hidden away, but instead be on the church website. Creating a culture of respect for them today will avoid a massive crisis two years from now that can destroy a great deal of hard work.

- Provide for appropriate financial oversight. Embezzlement or improper reimbursements involve both a perpetrator and an overly-lax congregational oversight group. When it hits the newspaper, the congregation may or may not recover.

- When gorillas are in the wild there are occasionally battles to determine which will be the Alpha Gorilla – the leader of the pack. When we see this happening in a congregation between two staff people, the entire Body of Christ has a responsibility to sit them down to explain that they are acting like large primates.

- There will always be gossips and manipulators with us. They will attack other laypeople and staff, but quite frequently, the lead pastor. A key elder, leader or staff person needs to publicly self-identify as the enforcer. If they see someone attacking the lead pastor or anyone else, they will quickly be in the attacker's living room talking about their behavior. This leader needs a personality and giftedness to be assertive without being abusive; loving but firm. This person and their role should be lifted up to the congregation. This cannot be the lead pastor.

- The entire elders group or administrative board in a healthy, united congregation need to self-identify as people who confront gossip and rumors. If there is evidence of sin by a pastor, let the formal process begin. If there is no evidence, we say, "I ask you as a Christian to remain silent on this issue." Every leader needs the spiritual maturity to lovingly confront gossip in the congregation and inappropriate staff behavior. When Brenda the choir director used the choir practice as a gossip session, she should have been confronted by the entire choir. It should never have become the pastor's problem.

If we want to stop the church from hurting people, we all have a role in making the hurting stop.

CHAPTER 15

Excommunication Is *Not* Burning at the Stake

> *I Corinthians 5:11*
> But now I am writing to you that you must not associate with anyone who claims to be a brother or sister but is sexually immoral or greedy, an idolater or slanderer, a drunkard or swindler. Do not even eat with such people.

Excommunication is a funny word. It's denotation, or exact meaning, is to remove someone from a social or organizational group. Businesses do it all the time when they fire someone for cause. Rotary clubs do it when someone's business ethics fall too low or they simply can't pay their quarterly dues. Kids get expelled from school for a time. The military gives dishonorable discharges. If I engage in a food fight at a restaurant the manager will probably tell me to never come back! People get excommunicated from groups and places in our society all the time. For some reason, we have stopped doing it in churches.

The connotation, or felt meaning, of the word 'excommunication' is quite sinister. It brings to mind the Spanish Inquisition and stretching someone on the rack. It is a downright medieval word, and who would want to return the church to that era?

Whether we respect the denotation or the connotation has tremendous consequences for local churches in the United States. If a local church avoids releasing certain gossips, manipulators and power brokers from membership, as most dying churches in the U.S. avoid doing, this church has almost no chance of turning around and reaching their community for Christ.

Who in their right mind would want to join a Rotary Club whose members were constantly in the local newspaper for shady business practices? Who would want their kids to attend a school where violence was rampant and the dean of students did nothing to bring order? Who in their right mind would want to join a local church where gossips, manipulators and power brokers ran the church, and infighting was constant and well known in the community? The answer? No one. A lack of discipline, even for the gravest of sins, is a church killer.

Even if there is no membership loss, the fact that no one new joins the church due to its reputation in the community for infighting means that local church is doomed. Slowly the membership will grow older and die.

At least a dozen pastors have told me their church is two or three deaths away from being able to grow. If Person X and Person Y will just get on with it and die this

EXCOMMUNICATION IS NOT BURNING AT THE STAKE

church would have a chance to reach its community and grow. I can hear in their voices that these pastors are only half kidding.

The main reason this increasingly popular pastoral joke is troubling is that a church that tolerates a manipulative gossip and wishes them to die is a church that will produce three manipulative gossips to replace the one – when he or she finally does get around to dying! Their death is highly unlikely to change the culture of the local church or its reputation in the community.

Only by bringing back a beautiful biblical concept, used successfully by businesses, non-religious clubs and schools throughout the world, will proper boundaries for behavior be re-established in the church.

Excommunication is about love. It is about restoration and purity. It is about caring deeply for a person and their eternal salvation while also caring for the purity of the congregation.

Before we get to excommunication, let's remember the words of Jesus in Matthew 18:15-17.

> "If your brother or sister sins, go and point out their fault, just between the two of you. If they listen to you, you have won them over. But if they will not listen, take one or two others along, so that 'every matter may be established by the testimony of two or three witnesses.' If they still refuse to listen, tell it to the church; and if they refuse to listen even to the church, treat them as you would a pagan or a tax collector."

Sin begins the discussion because there is no excommunication without a sin. None of the above should ever shock us. We are all sinners. It is our nature. It is why Christ died on the cross for us. Being shocked that an attender, a member or a leader has fallen to adultery or infighting in the church is an act of utter naiveté. Are we shocked when an anteater eats an ant or a possum gets into our garbage and leaves it all over the driveway? We can't be shocked because that's what anteaters and possums do! What do human beings do? We sin!

This is not promoting sin or going easy on it. It is simply admitting that it is the human condition. It is the little Pharisee within each of us that is shocked and appalled. The Pharisees said people should look upright and proper. Hide your sin from others because we dare not let them be known. A righteous appearance demands it. "The best way for a congregation to have a good reputation in the community is for it to be filled with perfect people," says the Pharisee. Unfortunately, this approach to sin never works.

Dietrich Bonhoeffer states it well:

> The pious fellowship permits no one to be a sinner. So everybody must conceal his sin from himself and from the fellowship. We dare not be sinners. Many Christians are unthinkably horrified when a real sinner is suddenly discovered among the righteous. So we remain alone with our sin, living in lies and hypocrisy. The fact is that we *are* sinners![46]

---

[46] Bonhoeffer, Dietrich, *Life Together*. Harper One, 1954. Page 110.

EXCOMMUNICATION IS NOT BURNING AT THE STAKE

Next comes the question: How does a fellowship of Christians, united together, deal with sin as it appears in a congregation. When manipulation and gossip, or any other painful sin, makes itself known, what do we do?

The answer? We love the sinner – as the Bible tells us to love them. We do everything possible to see the person restored to freedom from their sin, and we do everything we can to bring healing to those hurt. We look at the nature of God, who sent God's Son to die on the cross for us, and we do everything possible to restore the person to freedom from sin. God is long-suffering and so must we be.

As Matthew 18:15-17 shows us, we go to the gossip privately and let them know we are concerned about their actions. It takes sacrifice to be this courageous, but dying on the cross took courage and sacrifice, too. We love as Christ loved. In love and grace, we risk the relationship and we go privately to speak to the person. We love them enough to do so. No process of excommunication begins without this private step of love.

In the small minority of cases where the person does not accept responsibility for their sin, we find another courageous leader and we bring to their attention what we have dealt with privately up to this point. Possibly we are wrong and are misinterpreting the situation, or blowing it out of proportion. Possibly this courageous leader will look at us and tell us to let it go. This person should be someone who knows the Scriptures and shows the clear fruit of being a trusted Christian leader.

By the way, I'm not suggesting the pastor be bothered at this point. Up to and including step two is a job for the laity who love one another, and the church, enough to be sacrificial and courageous. If there is agreement, two go to the one who is sinning and address the issue lovingly, gracefully and directly.

Let's stop for a moment. The vast majority of sinners – which we all are – are really going to take a visit by two church lay leaders in their living room seriously. When presented with the evidence, a sane person is going to get humble, ask for forgiveness, and ask how they can be restored. At no point has the word excommunication been mentioned and in ninety-nine percent of cases the church just became less dysfunctional because the inappropriate actions of the gossip have been addressed. Inappropriate e-mails they have written or statements made to more than one person are clearly presented and the evidence is clear. An emotionally healthy person gets humble at this point.

In other words, excommunication is not our first step. If it is, then we truly do resemble the Spanish Inquisition and we are part of the problem of hurting people in the church and not a part of the biblical solution.

And then there is the one percent. When confronted by two loving, graceful, fully prayed-up church leaders with an abundance of evidence, the person does not repent. Evidence of adultery is presented and the person won't admit it. Clear evidence, in love, is presented regarding gossip or embezzlement and the person refuses to see it for the destructive power it has within a congregation.

Only two possibilities exist for this one percent of cases: The person needs a Christian mental health professional or they are an unrepentant sinner.

EXCOMMUNICATION IS NOT BURNING AT THE STAKE

Why would any organization, especially a local church, want an unbalanced person or an unrepentant sinner in church leadership? If the membership of the church elects elders or participates in decisions, such as new buildings or the selection of the lead pastor, why would we want an unbalanced person or an unrepentant sinner determining the future direction of the church?

In these rare cases the two bring their evidence and experiences with the person to the pastor, and after a proper time of exploration of the facts and probably a meeting with the person, it is brought before the full leadership of the church. Membership may be revoked – just like a business, a non-religious club or a school would do it.

There are two schools of thought regarding continued attendance at worship services. Some say this is an act of love to allow the person to continue to worship in the local church, but leadership and membership are removed. Others say they should be informed that they will be trespassing should they come to the church again.

The point is not worth debating until it actually happens. The percentage of people who will leave a church and never come back under these circumstances is very high. The number of people who will attempt to remain in that local church is tiny. The type of unrepentant sin (such as pedophilia), or the nature of their mental unbalance, makes this decision best done on a case-by case basis. It may be best to have them remain in the worshipping community. It may not be. The key is to remove them from any sense of church leadership or membership.

The other key is that the rest of the congregation will hear about it sooner or later. The leadership of the church can't openly discuss a matter of church discipline, but the congregation will probably know at some point. A sense of discipline and accountability will now be established. Boundaries and consequences, which we sinful human beings need in order to function together, will be restored to the congregation. This is one of the reasons we suspend kids from school. It communicates boundaries to the rest of the students.

Twelve people who were thinking of doing the same thing will think again. The level of dysfunction in the church will be reduced. We will never get it to zero because the church is full of human beings, but a healthy church never lets the dysfunction within the church get unnecessarily high or we simply cannot reach the community for Christ because our reputation has sunk too low.

Don't Forget the Final Step

Removing someone from leadership or membership is not medieval if it is done in love. Love for the person and their holiness, and love for the health of the church.

It is also love if someone is designated by the church leadership to reach out regularly to the expelled person, at least monthly. Our goal is restoration. It always has been. We want the mentally unhealthy to heal. We want the unrepentant sinner to repent and walk with the Lord.

The designated person, preferably someone who did not bring the issue to the church leadership, attempts to connect with the person month after month to meet their needs, pray with them and invite them to a restorative process.

Excommunication is *not* burning at the stake. It is a process that establishes boundaries for members and leaders and expresses grace and love to both the sinner and the church. It will also radically lower the number of people who get hurt in church.

A New Covenant

Twenty-five years ago I saw a church avoid biblical, loving accountability, and I brought it to one of my well-respected seminary professors, Dr. Ted Campbell. I ranted and raved about how destructive it was for this local church.

When I finally calmed down, Dr. Campbell let me know how common this was in local churches. He predicted in 1990 that it would damage local churches for generations to come until the church re-examines the issue of church discipline. He also said something else that was very profound.

If a pastor tries to bring someone to biblical accountability in a church with no covenant of accountability, the pastor will probably be removed and the culture of the church will not change. A new covenant of our life together needs to be established before we can start enforcement or it will simply be perceived as unexpected, humiliating and medieval. It will simply be time to change pastors.

For this reason, the wise pastor takes this chapter and realizes it was written for the laity. He or she prepares a sermon series on biblical accountability as part of preaching through the entirety of the Scriptures. A wise pastor asks the leadership to write a covenant together over a series of meetings that is later signed by all.

A wise pastor gathers laity together from the different areas of the church and shares the leadership's new covenant with the larger group. After months of discussion and input, a membership covenant is formed. After a Sunday where the laity present it to the laity, everyone is invited to sign it as they leave the worship service.

An unwise pastor shakes the dust off the 100-year-old denominational book and starts enforcing it as if the congregation has agreed to it or even read it. Membership vows that include vague lines such as, "I agree to support the covenant of our denomination," are unwise. New members, and the existing membership, need to see what the covenant looks like and agree to live under it before enforcement can begin.

As I finish writing this chapter, I am overhearing a phone conversation my son is having with a friend. He's talking about the three people who got kicked out of the Army during his Basic Training this summer at Fort Leonard Wood, Missouri. He reminded the person on the other end of the line that the expectations had been clearly communicated during the first week of training. My son concluded his comments with, "We sure learned from those three what not to do."

It is deeply regrettable and painful when people hurt others in the church. It is inexcusable when it becomes an acceptable, normal part of the life of the church, over and against the words of Scripture.

EXCOMMUNICATION IS NOT BURNING AT THE STAKE

Take a look at the following Scriptures from various biblical authors, all of whom wrote with the inspiration of the Holy Spirit. In the lines below, write your thoughts about each passage. Is setting certain persons outside the church, until they repent and return, biblical? Would returning to this approach keep churches from hurting people right and left?

2 Thessalonians 3:6
_____
_____
_____
_____
_____

Leviticus 18:29
_____
_____
_____
_____
_____

1 Corinthians 5:1-2
_____
_____
_____
_____
_____

1 Timothy 1:20 (Handing a person over to Satan for a time is understood as removing a person from fellowship.)

_____
_____
_____
_____
_____

Matthew 18:15-18 (To be treated as a Gentile or a Tax Collector means to exclude from fellowship.)

_____
_____
_____
_____
_____

CHAPTER 16

If You Have Been Hurt

Psalm 23:1-3a
The LORD is my shepherd, I lack nothing.
He makes me lie down in green pastures,
he leads me beside quiet waters,
he refreshes my soul.

The cover of this book shows the statue called *And Jesus Wept*. It is found in Oklahoma City across the street from the federal building that was destroyed by a domestic terrorist in 1995, costing the lives of 168 people.

Jesus certainly did not cause this event any more than he caused the hurt we have experienced at the hands of American Civil Religion run amok. Jesus weeps when he thinks of the bombing, and he weeps when he thinks of the hurt that tens of millions of people have gone through because some groups, masquerading as churches, have deeply hurt others.

How can I compare the hurt from American Civil Religion with the death of 168 people? Easily. Because tens of millions of people have been hurt, an incalculable number of people have turned away from the faith and will not be with the Lord in heaven. An incalculable number of people see the pain caused by American Civil Religion and never consider faith in Jesus Christ. The eternal consequences of churches that hurt are tremendous.

People being hurt by American Civil Religion – which is not very civil – has become the number one reason why people leave the faith or do not consider it in the first place.[47]

And Jesus Wept.

There is a natural human and completely understandable reaction to being hurt by American Civil Religion. We say to ourselves and to others, "I will never enter the doors of that church again!" Depending on the circumstances we may be completely justified.

Then we are tempted by our enemy to go on and make another statement. "I will never enter the doors of any church, ever again."

And Jesus Wept.

The Faithful Church is a place to worship God. We have built into the very fibers of our being the need to worship God. To deny it, and to forego worship in any church, because of hurt, brings tears to God's eyes.

The Faithful Church is a place to be prepared for service. Within the very fibers of our being is a desire to serve others and to help the least of these. We need to be prepared, discipled and strengthened for this work. When we

---

[47] Krejcir, Richard J., *Why Churches Fail: Part I*. At http://www.churchleadership.org/apps/articles/default.asp?blogid=4545&url=10&view=post&articleid=42339&fldKeywords=&fldAuthor=&fldTopic=0 July 19, 2015

are not, and our lives become focused only on our close families and ourselves, Jesus weeps.

The Faithful Church is a place to show us how to enjoy the great spiritual disciplines of the faith: prayer, fasting, reading or hearing the Scriptures, Holy Communion, listening to praise music during the week and so many others which bring us into sweet spiritual intimacy with God. When we don't, God weeps because this was the original reason God created us. God doesn't need a daily relationship with us, but God so very much desires it.

The Faithful Church is a place to learn the Scriptures and apply them to our lives. God sent the prophets and the Son to reveal God's Word to us. Jesus weeps when we ignore this revelation simply because we were hurt.

The Faithful Church is a place to be in fellowship with others who worship the Lord. We were designed to be in relationship with God, but also with each other. We are designed to love and to be loved. Jesus weeps when we choose the unnecessary path of loneliness and depression.

The Faithful Church is a place to be transformed and to become better people, a more ethical people. Our society needs tens of millions of people with an ethical foundation. When our society does not have this, Jesus weeps.

I've been hurt, just like you. I have faced the temptation to never enter the church again. I simply have a set of experiences you probably don't have.

I've met Cuban Christians from the unregistered church who walked two hours in the heat and humidity to be in a Faithful Church. No one would do that for

American Civil Religion week after week. Even after they were arrested and imprisoned for two years, they got out of jail and started walking to church again.

I've met Christians among the Toba Indians who walked through the Chaco of Paraguay because their cacique (chief) had told them the Word of God was to be preached and a fellowship meal and celebration was to follow. There were a lot of poisonous snakes between where they lived and where the Faithful Church met. They did those long walks anyway.

There is so much beauty in the Faithful Church and so much that we were designed to need. It is part of completing us and forming us and allowing us the privilege of full worship.

If a two-hour car ride stands between you and a Faithful Church, drive it. If some research into healthy churches is needed on your part to find one, do the research. If overcoming the fear of being a first-time visitor is your obstacle, jump over it! Visit until you find a place to worship, to develop, to grow and to serve.

The Faithful Church is often found in a living room with a small group Bible study where believers hear the Word, open up to one another, and feel their loneliness fade. If you can't find a Faithful Church near you, start a Bible study in your living room.

Some will choose to stay in American Civil Religion and fight for change. If that is God's call on your life, you have my respect. Just make sure you spend enough time in a Faithful Church atmosphere from time to time that you continue to have the strength to carry on.

Others will choose to leave American Civil Religion as I have. It is not church shopping. It is recognizing how weak and corrupt American Civil Religion has become and figuring out what the bare minimum requirements are for you to stay in a church. Possibly you are also concerned about raising your family in a Faithful Church so they are not hurt as you and I have been.

In the next and final chapter, you will be asked to define an ideal church, as well as the bare minimum you need from a church in order to stay within it. Have a pen or pencil handy. This is where it all comes together as you determine your personal definition of the Faithful Church.

Forgiveness

For those of us who have been hurt, we also need to forgive. Christ died on the cross to forgive us of our sin. We are also asked to forgive others of the sin that brought pain into our lives. God desires us to be free from the slavery of unforgiveness.

From the Sermon on the Mount we read a terrifying concept:

> For if you forgive other people when they sin against you, your heavenly Father will also forgive you. But if you do not forgive others their sins, your Father will not forgive your sins. (Matthew 6:14-15)

Within the same Sermon on the Mount comes the primary way in which we exercise this forgiveness:

> But I tell you, love your enemies and pray for those who persecute you, that you may be children of your Father in heaven. He causes his sun to rise on the evil and the good, and sends rain on the righteous and the unrighteous. (Matthew 5:44-45)

Who is it within the Church who has hurt you? Use a separate sheet of paper or the final blank pages of this book if you need more space.

_____
_____
_____
_____
_____
_____
_____

Before God, what steps do you need to take to forgive them and to be set free? (Praying for them, speaking with them, retreats, journaling, etc.)

_____
_____
_____
_____
_____
_____
_____
_____

CHAPTER 17

For You, What Are the Traits of a Faithful Church?

Matthew 28:19-20
"Therefore go and make disciples of all nations, baptizing them in the name of the Father and of the Son and of the Holy Spirit, and teaching them to obey everything I have commanded you. And surely I am with you always, to the very end of the age."

Where can I grow in my faith and serve? Where can my family grow in its faith and serve? What are the traits of a church where people are far less likely to get hurt? Consider the following as you come to your own conclusions to these questions. Use the lines after the list to add, subtract or modify it.

Please be careful about placing "Music I like," or "Preaching I like," on your list. This sort of consumer-oriented approach to looking for a church has pushed churches to be shallow and place all their energy into a spectacular show on Sunday morning with little or no energy going into discipleship, spiritual growth, service and leadership development.

The Faithful Church is about worship, but it is also about learning the Word of God. It is about growth in numbers, but only if people are growing spiritually as well.

1. Define the ideal church by placing check marks in the boxes.

2. Go back and circle those areas that are absolutely necessary in order for you or your family to worship, to connect and to serve in a local church. What are the bare minimums for you in order to choose a congregation or to stay in a congregation?

I want to help my church become a Faithful Church that:

☐ Believes in the Old and New Testament

☐ Believes in Jesus Christ as the only Savior

☐ Trains and chooses leadership carefully and not casually.

☐ Has a clear Discipleship process that the pastor or staff can tell me about or show me on paper.

☐ Is involved in and is making the community a better place.

FOR YOU, WHAT ARE THE TRAITS OF A FAITHFUL CHURCH?

☐ Is involved in outreach to the region and to the world.

☐ While I am still in the world working, studying and being with those who do not know the Lord, the church is a sanctuary where I can find community and fellowship. It is not a dangerous place with gossips on the loose.

☐ Those in the church community are willing to gracefully confront me if I stray from the path of Christ.

☐ The worship service strengthens me and those around me and helps me to be in a spirit of worship all week long.

☐ If I, or a member of my family, does not know our Spiritual Gifts and areas where we can serve the Lord with passion, the church can help us discover them and allow us to serve.

☐ Has a unified staff all pulling the same direction.

☐ The lead pastor is a visionary leader and not a dictator.

☐ When I ask to see financial statements, they are provided and I feel confident the Lord's money is being used in a wise and transparent way.

- ☐ Has a pastor who is praying, fasting and retreating, or can tell me about other Spiritual Disciplines which draw the pastor close to the Lord.

- ☐ Where gossip and manipulation are dealt with lovingly and gracefully, but they are dealt with.

- ☐ Is a church that prays regularly, often and in many ways.

In your definition of the Faithful Church, what would you add to the above list?

☐ _____
_____
_____

☐ _____
_____
_____

☐ _____
_____
_____

☐ _____
_____

FOR YOU, WHAT ARE THE TRAITS OF A FAITHFUL CHURCH?

☐ _____
_____
_____
_____

☐ _____
_____
_____
_____

Once again, the exercise is to:

1. Define the ideal church by placing check marks in the boxes.

2. Go back and circle those areas that are absolutely necessary in order for you or your family to worship, to connect and to serve in a local church. What are the bare minimums for you in order to choose a congregation or to stay in a congregation?

Now check the boxes below that apply to you personally. Some may need a week or more to make these decisions. You may check more than one.

☐ I've been hurt very badly by a church. I need to seek out someone to help me in a journey of forgiveness and healing.

☐ I haven't been attending a church but I know I need to in order to fulfill my calling as a Christian. I'm going to take my bare minimum list of requirements for a Faithful Church, interview pastors and find a new spiritual home where I am far less likely to be hurt.

☐ My current congregation meets my bare minimum list and I'm going to work to see it get closer to the ideal list for a faithful church.

☐ My current congregation does not meet my bare minimum list. I've seen too many people get hurt here, including me and my family, and I don't believe the congregation will change any time soon. It is time to start praying and looking for a healthy, Faithful Church. I'm not casually going church shopping like a consumer. I am simply respecting what I feel are biblical bare minimums.

Even though American Civil Religion has hurt you in the past, you are now much more prepared to find a healthy, Faithful Church or to help make your church into a healthy, Faithful Church.

Blessings and peace on you and your family as you worship and serve the Lord.

Remember, God loves the Church. She is the Bride of Christ. Let's make her a beautiful bride and keep nudging toward the biblical, ideal definition of the church.

APPENDIX

Potential Questions for Accountability Groups

Regularly asking one another some of these questions can help Christian leaders and disciples stay pure as we serve within a culture that has become anything but pure.

John Wesley's Small Group Questions:
1. Am I consciously or unconsciously creating the impression that I am better than I am? In other words, am I a hypocrite?

2. Am I honest in all my acts and words, or do I exaggerate?

3. Do I confidentially pass on to another what was told me in confidence?

4. Am I a slave to dress, friends, work, or habits?

5. Am I self-conscious, self-pitying, or self-justifying?

6. Does the Bible live in me today?

7. Do I give it time to speak to me every day?

8. Am I enjoying prayer?

9. When did I last speak to someone about my faith?

10. Do I pray about the money I spend?

11. Do I get to bed on time and get up on time?

12. Do I disobey God in anything?

13. Do I insist upon doing something about which my conscience is uneasy?

14. Am I defeated in any part of my life?

15. Am I jealous, impure, critical, irritable, touchy or distrustful?

16. How do I spend my spare time?

17. Am I proud?

18. Do I thank God that I am not as other people, especially as the Pharisee who despised the publican?

19. Is there anyone whom I fear, dislike, disown, criticize, hold resentment toward or disregard? If so, what am I going to do about it?

20. Do I grumble and complain constantly?

21. Is Christ real to me?

Wesley's Band Meeting Questions:

1. What known sins have you committed since our last meeting?

2. What temptations have you met with?

3. How were you delivered?

4. What have you thought, said, or done, of which you doubt whether it be sin or not?

5. Have you nothing you desire to keep secret?

Reference: *John Wesley's Class Meetings: a Model for Making Disciples*, by D. Michael Henderson, Evangel Publishing House, 1997, pp. 118-9

Chuck Swindoll's Pastoral Accountability Questions:

In his book, *The Body*, Chuck Colson lists the questions used by Chuck Swindoll.

1. Have you been with a man or woman anywhere this past week that might be seen as compromising?

2. Have any of your financial dealings lacked integrity?

3. Have you exposed yourself to any sexually explicit material?

4. Have you spent adequate time in Bible study and prayer?

5. Have you given priority time to your family?

6. Have you fulfilled the mandates of your calling?

7. Have you just lied to me?

Neil Cole:

1. What is the condition of your soul?

2. What sin do you need to confess?

3. What have you held back from God that you need to surrender?

4. Is there anything that has dampened your zeal for Christ?

5. Who have you talked with about Christ this week?

10 Additional Questions

1. Have you been a testimony this week to the greatness of Jesus Christ with both your words and actions?

2. Have you been exposed to sexually alluring material or allowed your mind to entertain inappropriate thoughts about someone who is not your spouse this week?

3. Have you lacked any integrity in your financial dealings this week, or coveted something that does not belong to you?

4. Have you been honoring, understanding and generous in your important relationships this past week?

5. Have you damaged another person by your words, either behind their back or face-to-face?

6. Have you given in to an addictive behavior this week? Explain.

7. Have you continued to remain angry toward another?

8. Have you secretly wished for another's misfortune so that you might excel?

9. Did you finish your reading this week and hear from the Lord? What are you going to do about it?

10. Have you been completely honest with us?

Notes

Notes

About the Author

Dr. Dan White is a former church planter in Paraguay, Peru, and the United States. As a missionary, he toured thirty to forty churches in the U.S. during each fundraising year before coming back to the U.S. to pastor. He is an Adjunct Assistant Professor of Practical Theology at Fuller Seminary and an Adjunct Professor at Wesley Seminary at Indiana Wesleyan University (IWU). His M.Div. is from Duke and his D.Min. is from Fuller. His wife, Gloria, is a Registered Pharmacist. Dan may be reached at dan.white@indwes.edu.

www.ingramcontent.com/pod-product-compliance
Lightning Source LLC
Chambersburg PA
CBHW031346040426
42444CB00005B/201